The High Protein Cook[illegible] [illegible]ealth During Cance[illegible]

This cookbook was developed by its authors at the University of Alberta.

Conceptualization, supervision, and resources – Dr. Carla Prado
Recipe design – Hillary Wilson and volunteers
Recipe testing – Anissa Armet, Hillary Wilson, and numerous volunteers
Props, food styling, photography – Anissa Armet
Cover page photography – Anissa Armet
Authors' bios photography – Rafaella Roriz
Design and layout – Julie Rohr and Bueno Design
Editorial manager – Anita Grande-Armet

Human Nutrition Research Unit
Li Ka Shing Centre for Health Research Innovation
University of Alberta
Edmonton, Alberta T6G 2P5
https://hnru.ualberta.ca/

Prado Lab
2-2021 Li Ka Shing Centre for Health Research Innovation
University of Alberta
Edmonton, Alberta T6G 2P5
https://www.drcarlaprado.com/

ISBN – 978-1-55195-476-9
Printed and bound in Canada.

Suggested citation –
Wilson HA, Armet AM, and Prado CM. 2022. The High Protein Cookbook for Muscle During Cancer Treatment. http://openeducationalberta.ca/proteincookbookforcancer

Download a free copy of this cookbook online at:
https://doi.org/10.7939/r3-sht5-h941

ADDITIONAL RELATED EDUCATIONAL MATERIALS:

We are committed to providing educational resources, and we invite you to check out some additional materials we have produced.

- Animated video: The Importance of Nutrition to Prevent and Treat Low Muscle Mass

https://www.youtube.com/watch?v=pDSX_jaDCDM (version in English)

https://www.youtube.com/watch?v=QVZ9MLrVt8I (version in French)

- Presentation and infographic: Adding Protein to our Diets

https://compassionhouse.org/the-importance-of-nutrition-protein/

- Scientific publication discussing the importance of animal protein:

Ford KL, Arends J, Atherton PJ, Engelen MPKJ, Gonçalves TJM, Laviano A, Lobo DN, Phillips SM, Ravasco P, Deutz NEP, Prado CM. The importance of protein sources to support muscle anabolism in cancer: An expert group opinion. Clin Nutr. 2022 Jan;41(1):192-201.

IMPORTANT NOTE

As mentioned later in this book, nutritional needs may change among patients. Check with your dietitian, nurse, or doctor if the recipes included here are safe for you.

Consuming a variety of foods is essential to get the nutrients needed during cancer treatment; this includes a combination of animal- and plant-based protein sources. Registered dietitians are healthcare professionals who can help assess your unique needs and design targeted strategies to guide nutrition care during your journey in receiving cancer treatment.

Dr. Carla Prado

Professor, University of Alberta
Director, Human Nutrition Research Unit
Campus Alberta Innovation Program Chair in Nutrition, Food and Health

   @drcarlaprado

Nutrition is powerful! It can be used to help people—including those with cancer—live longer with better health. This cookbook is particularly focused on muscle health, which is related to the amount and type of protein in our diets. People with cancer need more protein than those who are healthy, and animal protein sources are particularly important for building muscle mass; these include, among others, beef, pork, chicken, fish, eggs, milk, and cheese. Our High Protein Cookbook for Muscle Health During Cancer Treatment includes 66 high protein recipes for breakfast, lunch, dinner, and snacks to help patients increase their protein intake for muscle health.

This nonprofit cookbook is our gift to you. Here, we combine two of our passions: nutrition and serving our community. We hope this is distributed to thousands of patients; we have published this cookbook as a freely downloadable resource to achieve this goal.

Enjoy the delicious recipes and beautiful pictures we have selected, and we hope that this book serves as a constant reminder that Muscle Matters!

WHERE DID THE IDEA COME FROM?

I was inspired to initiate this project in 2017 during a visit to Dr. Aoife Ryan's laboratory at the University College Cork in Ireland. At that time, Dr. Ryan gave me a copy of her first cookbook for people with cancer, titled: Good Nutrition for Cancer Recovery. I was not only in awe of the quality of the book but, above all, her vision and initiative to create this nutritional educational resource for patients. Her cookbook was focused on high protein and high calorie recipes for those experiencing cancer-induced weight loss. As many of the patients we were working with in Canada would benefit from high protein but normal calorie recipes, I decided to adapt her idea to meet their needs. The aim was to increase protein intake for muscle health (prevent muscle loss and promote muscle gain) but without higher calorie recipes. I invited two nutrition students and our late friend, Julie Rohr, who effortlessly volunteered their time towards the completion of this project. Together, we recruited several additional volunteers who helped us achieve our goal (see Acknowledgements).

WHY FOCUS ON PROTEIN? MUSCLE MATTERS!

Protein is essential for muscle maintenance and growth. It also helps our immune system, healing, and recovery. My research looks at the importance of muscle mass for patients with cancer. Low muscle mass can happen at any stage of cancer, from early to advanced, and is associated with severe side effects due to chemotherapy, cancer progression, surgical complications, and shorter survival times, among other problems. Therefore, preventing and reversing low muscle mass has the potential to improve health outcomes and survival.

While treating cancer and exercising are important for muscle health, nutrition is an essential piece of the puzzle because it supplies the nutrients and substances we need to build muscle. This includes protein, which is the main building block of muscle.

Hillary A. Wilson, RD

Hillary is currently a medical student at the University of Alberta. She completed her BSc. in Nutrition in 2018 and worked as a registered dietitian prior to beginning medical school. Her passion for wellness and food, along with a desire to improve the lives of others, motivated her to follow this career path as well as her involvement in the development of this cookbook. Cooking for herself is a regular part of her routine, and as a busy student she appreciates the value of simple, healthy, and tasty recipes.

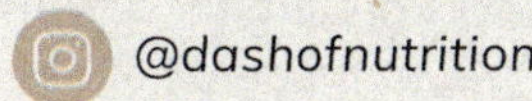 RD

@dashofnutrition

Anissa is a registered dietitian and PhD candidate in Nutrition and Metabolism at the University of Alberta. She has a particular passion for food styling and photography, and believes that you should "eat with your eyes" first. This is why Anissa was brought on to test, photograph, and edit all of the recipes included in this cookbook.

Anissa truly believes that nutrition can and should be used as a first-line therapy. She hopes these delicious and nutritious recipes help people realize how protein rich foods can help nourish muscle mass, especially during cancer treatment.

Julie A. Rohr

In Memoriam

Julie was an inspiring mom, wife, daughter, sister, and friend, whose legacy lives on. She had leiomyosarcoma, a rare incurable cancer of soft muscle tissue. She surpassed her cancer prognosis by five years. She was a dear friend of Dr. Prado's laboratory, and was passionate about the importance of nutrition for patients with cancer and people connecting over meals to support one another.

Julie was an advocate, writer, photographer, creator, and served in many volunteering endeavours. In 2019, she would add 'cookbook graphic designer' to this list. We shared our vision and goal for this cookbook and Julie immediately volunteered her time and talent to serve as our graphic designer. Her initial layout designs brought our recipes and photos to life.

We are extremely grateful for Julie's vision and contributions to this cookbook. As a strong believer in the importance of nutrition and health, Julie was eager to see this project to completion so that it could help others experiencing cancer. We dedicate this book to her and hope her life story will continue to inspire and bless countless throughout the world. We thank Julie's family for allowing us to honour her here.

Please visit https://www.julierohr.org/ to learn more about Julie's legacy.

ACKNOWLEDGEMENTS

The development of this cookbook, including creating its content and testing its recipes, was only possible with the support of the following individuals (in alphabetical order): Anne Caretero, Guilin Chen, Jarson Costa, Reena Duke, Sherin Fernandes, Victoria Ferraz, Rebecca Fox, Michelle Mackenzie, Yuzhu Mao, Bruna Ramos Da Silva, Felicia Sim, Nilian Souza, and Marisa Trinca.

We would also like to thank the following registered dietitians for submitting recipes to this cookbook: Jennifer Black, Katherine Ford, Lindsay Lee, and Louise Lacanilao.

A special thank you to Anita Grande-Armet who was involved in numerous aspects of this project, especially recipe testing and editing the cookbook, and selflessly dedicated her time towards ensuring its completion.

We would also like to thank Brenda McCullough, who shared our vision and supported us with advice and guidance along the way.

We thank the University of Alberta Library, especially Michelle Brailey, for assistance in publishing this cookbook online (on Pressbooks) and in print.

Finally, we would like to thank the University of Alberta's Faculty of Agricultural, Life and Environmental Sciences for their support of this cookbook, allowing us to give back to our community. Thank you to Katherine Irwin and Cynthia Strawson for your support.

Funding for this project was partially provided by the Campus Alberta Innovation Program.

FOREWORD

When I first qualified as a dietitian twenty years ago, I spent eight wonderful years in a large University teaching hospital in Dublin working in oncology and gastrointestinal surgery. I met many patients who struggled to eat, and many experienced swallowing difficulties. Back then, we thought that if patients simply ate more food they would gain weight and do better. They were given high-protein, high fat, high-calorie dietary advice and black-and-white leaflets of information of what to eat and what to avoid. I remember feeling frustrated and disappointed when so many patients would continue to lose weight at follow up appointments and began to question what I was doing! My PhD work led me to a greater understanding of the complexities of nutritional status in patients with cancer and the impact that poor nutrition had on outcomes.

I, and many colleagues internationally, have been inspired by the research of Prof Carla Prado at the University of Alberta. Her work has dramatically changed the way that dietitians and doctors think about weight loss in cancer. Through evaluation of CT scans, Prof Prado was the first to notice that muscle was lost in large quantities following a cancer diagnosis and that this impacted how patients tolerated chemotherapy. Much research on this topic has been done over the past 10-15 years internationally, and what we now know is that cancer-induced weight loss affects 30-80% of patients and is associated with poorer tolerance to chemotherapy, impaired quality of life, more frequent hospital admissions, and reduced survival. The research of Prof Carla Prado and others has shown that if patients eat enough energy (calories) and aim for 25-30 grams of protein per meal, they can better their chances of maintaining their muscle mass on cancer treatment. This means they have a better chance of tolerating treatment, including chemotherapy, radiotherapy, and/or surgery. The question is: how can a patient achieve these nutritional targets?

While many cancer patients eat as well as they can, they are unfortunately dealing with a series of complex changes in their metabolism. Cancer cells, through their interaction with the immune system, cause 'chemical messengers' to be produced in the body, which can cause appetite loss, inflammation, and rapid loss of muscle. It is a significant challenge to get some patients to stabilize their weight and an even greater challenge to help them to regain lost weight and muscle. We urgently need simple patient resources to help patients eat better in their homes and minimize these changes in their body composition.

Having spent many years writing scientific articles (that only fellow scientists would ever read), I decided in 2012 it was time to translate what we knew about nutrition into a simple cookbook for patients with cancer and their families. I was lucky to receive funding to work on this project and, in 2013, we launched *'Good Nutrition for Cancer Recovery'* in Ireland, which is a free high-protein high-calorie cookbook for patients who are experiencing weight loss while undergoing treatment for cancer. We went on to publish cookbooks for swallowing difficulties in cancer, and cookbooks on healthy eating for cancer survivors in the years that followed. In total, we distributed over 50,000 free cookbooks to Irish patients. The impact of this work far outweighs any scientific articles I will ever write as it directly helps cancer patients, their families, and health care professionals. While our books have won a number of awards, I was always conscious that they were only available in Ireland. I am delighted that that Prof Prado's team at the University of Alberta has developed their own high-protein cookbook, and I congratulate them on this enormous effort. This cookbook translates what scientists know about protein and good nutrition into easy-to-prepare, nutritious meals that can help slow the loss of weight and muscle mass. I have no doubt it will be well-received and greatly appreciated by patients and their carers. I am hopeful more countries will follow suit to make evidence-based nutritional resources more accessible.

Aoife Ryan, PhD, RD
Senior Lecturer in Human Nutrition & Dietetics
University College Cork
Ireland

ENDORSEMENTS -
University of Alberta Human Nutrition Professors

Nutrition plays a key role in providing the best patient care during and beyond cancer treatment. The goal of *The High Protein Cookbook for Muscle Health During Cancer Treatment* is to empower patients to prepare high protein meals. This cookbook is evidence-informed and filled with dozens of enjoyable and nutritious recipes for people undergoing cancer treatment.

One in two Albertans will be diagnosed with cancer in their lifetime. Protein in particular is especially important for patients with cancer to ensure their muscle mass – the body's suit of armour that protects against poor health outcomes – is maintained. The recipes in this cookbook are high in protein and other essential nutrients, equipping patients with the ingredients necessary not just for strong muscles, but a strong, healthy immune system as well.

The goal of Human Nutrition research at the University of Alberta is to explore the links between all aspects of nutrition and human health, with the ultimate goal of preventing diseases and enhancing the quality of life. *The High Protein Cookbook for Muscle Health During Cancer Treatment* and its easy-to-follow recipes align with this strategy as it encourages Albertans experiencing cancer to think of food as another type of powerful medicine. The recipes and related content in this cookbook were designed by registered dietitians. We would highly recommend this resource for patients who are searching for delicious meal and snack ideas to help strengthen them on their health journey.

Catherine J. Field, PhD, RD
Canada Research Chair in Human Nutrition and Metabolism
University of Alberta, Edmonton
AB Canada

Vera C. Mazurak, PhD
Professor, Human Nutrition
University of Alberta, Edmonton
AB Canada

ENDORSEMENTS - Dean, Faculty of Agricultural, Life and Environmental Sciences, University of Alberta

At the University of Alberta's Faculty of Agricultural, Life & Environmental Sciences, part of our core mission is to turn science into solutions for the public good. Each day our faculty members, undergraduate and graduate students, and staff members contribute to and support research that will eventually become these solutions.

The *High Protein Cookbook for Muscle Health During Cancer Treatment* is just one example of the fulfillment of this incredibly important value. Professor Carla Prado, Anissa Armet, Hillary Wilson, and other researchers and registered dietitians at the University of Alberta have created this important and tangible resource to support the community with their expertise. The team has made this book widely available and easily accessible so that it has the potential to help as many people as possible.

I am certain that this work, on the heels of a number of other amazing contributions coming out of the Human Nutrition Research Unit as well as many other facilities, centres, and individuals at the University of Alberta, will continue to inspire further solutions to the issues that we face now and into the future. I am incredibly impressed and inspired by the work that has gone into the *High Protein Cookbook for Muscle Health During Cancer Treatment* and hope that you will find it just as powerful and useful.

Stanford Blade, PhD
Dean, Faculty of Agricultural, Life and Environmental Sciences
University of Alberta, Edmonton
AB Canada

IMPORTANT INFORMATION

Patients with cancer may have different nutritional and physiological needs, and this may also be influenced by other conditions/diseases. Please consult a member of your health care team to ensure the information hereby provided is appropriate and safe for you.

FOOD SAFETY

If you are receiving medical treatment that weakens your immune system, you may need to take additional precautions when cooking to reduce the risk of infection. Everyone can benefit from practicing food safety techniques. For example, wash your hands before and after touching raw meat, and do not use plates, utensils, or cutting boards again that have touched raw meat before washing and sanitizing them.

We encourage using a meat thermometer to check that foods are cooked to a safe internal temperature. Please visit Health Canada's website for a list of safe cooking temperatures for different foods: https://www.canada.ca/en/health-canada/services/general-food-safety-tips/safe-internal-cooking-temperatures.html

For more information on food safety, please visit: https://www.canada.ca/en/health-canada/services/general-food-safety-tips.html

Leftovers can be an easy way to have a quick, healthy meal in minutes. It is generally safe to store leftovers in the fridge for up to 3 days. If you would like to store them for longer, individually portion and place in the freezer for up to 3 months.

NUTRITIONAL INFORMATION TABLES IN RECIPES

Nutritional information was derived from analyzing the recipes as written using a validated software (ESHA Food Processor®). Generic brands of ingredients and Canadian Nutrient File data were used when available.

Portion sizes are meant to be used as a guide. If the portion sizes are adjusted, please note that the nutrition information provided in the recipe will need to be changed as well.

SEASONINGS AND MODIFICATIONS

These recipes were created to be appropriate for people with a variety of health conditions and dietary modifications. Therefore, salt has not been included as an ingredient in these recipes. If advised by your healthcare provider, we welcome you to season to taste.

We also encourage you to be flexible when making these recipes and use ingredients that are in season and available. Please note that any modifications will alter the nutrition information provided in the recipes.

Breakfast

Lunch

Dinner

Snacks

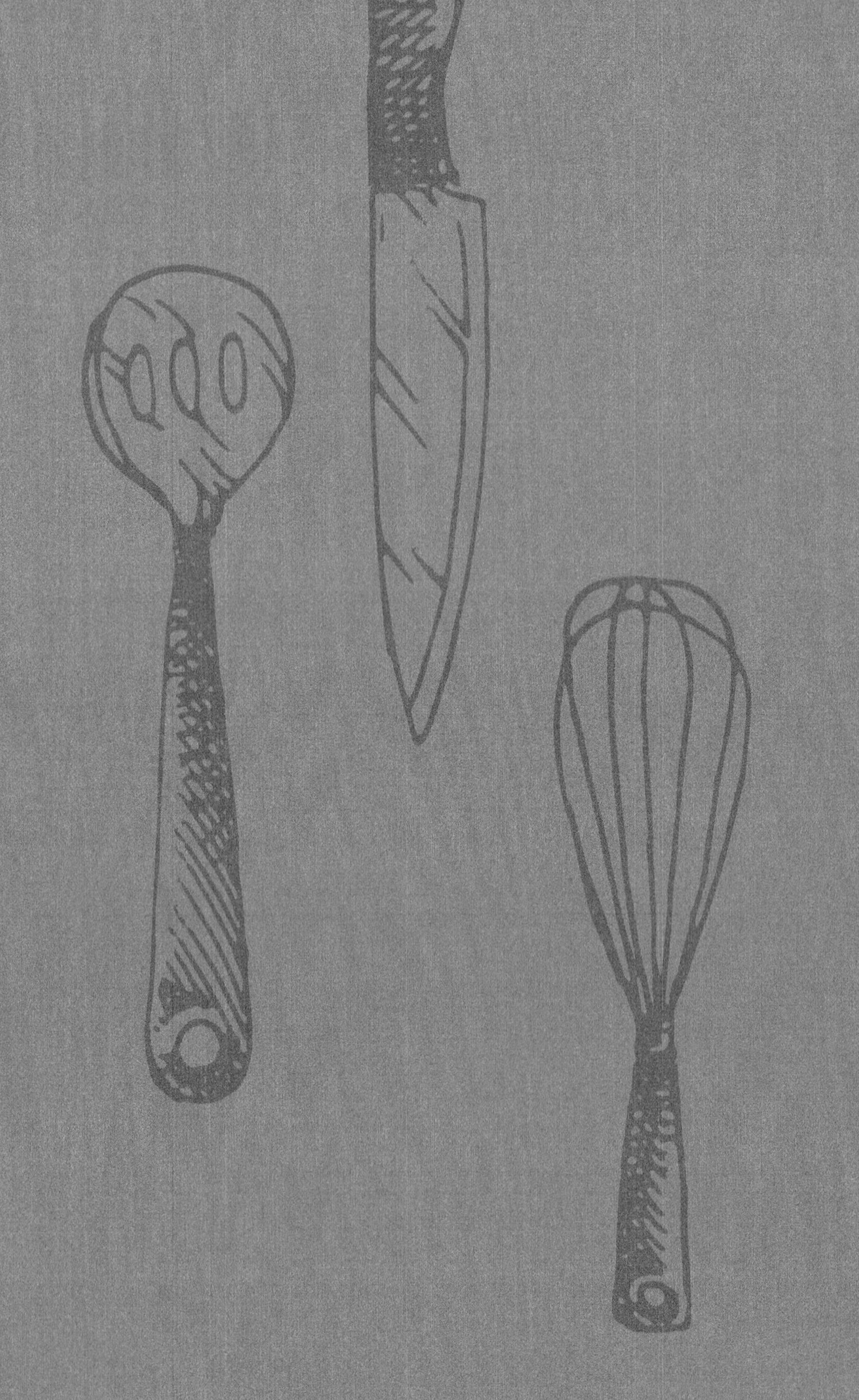

Breakfast
RECIPES

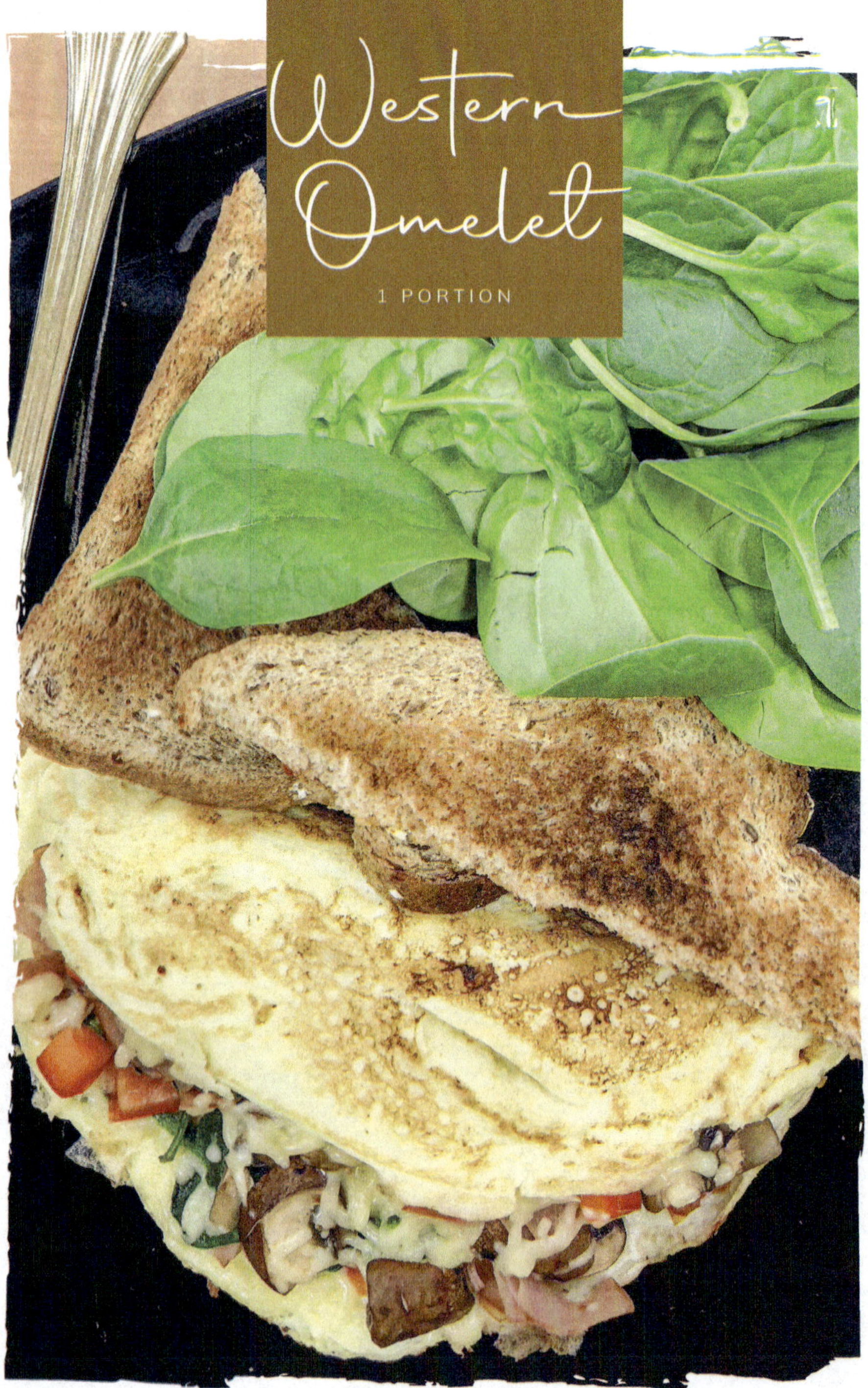

Western Omelet

1 PORTION

 **PREP TIME:** 5 minutes |  **TOTAL TIME:** 15 minutes

INGREDIENTS:

- 2 large eggs
- ⅛ tsp black pepper
- 2 medium button mushrooms, sliced
- ¼ cup fresh spinach
- 4 cherry tomatoes, quartered
- 1 oz (28 g) extra lean low sodium ham
- 1 tsp (5 mL) canola oil
- 1 Tbsp. low fat cheddar cheese, shredded
- 1 slice whole wheat bread, toasted

DIRECTIONS:

- Whisk eggs and black pepper together in a bowl.
- Heat 2 Tbsp. (30 mL) water in a small non-stick skillet over medium-high heat.
- Add mushrooms and cook for 5 minutes or until tender.
- Add the spinach, tomatoes, and ham; stir until spinach is wilted.
- Remove the filling from the skillet; set aside.
- Heat oil in the same skillet over medium-high heat.
- Pour in whisked eggs. As eggs set around the edge of the skillet, gently push cooked portions toward the centre of the skillet with a spatula. Tilt and rotate skillet to allow uncooked egg to flow into empty spaces.
- When eggs are almost set on the surface but still look moist, cover half of the omelet with filling. Slip spatula under unfilled side; fold over onto filled half.
- Cook for a minute, then slide the omelet onto the plate.
- Garnish with shredded cheese. Serve with toast.

NUTRIENT PER PORTION	CALORIES	PROTEIN	CARBOHYDRATES	FAT	FIBRE	SODIUM
	357 kcal	27g	19g	20g	4g	625mg

Huevos Rancheros Breakfast Wraps

CONTRIBUTED BY: LINDSAY LEE, RD

1 PORTION

 **PREP TIME:** 5 minutes |  **TOTAL TIME:** 10 minutes

INGREDIENTS:

- 1 tsp (5 mL) canola oil
- 2 large eggs
- ½ cup no sodium added black beans, drained and rinsed
- ½ tsp chili powder
- 2 5-inch (13 cm) soft corn tortillas
- 1 medium green onion, thinly sliced
- 1 medium tomato, chopped
- 2 Tbsp. low fat Monterey Jack cheese, shredded

DIRECTIONS:

- Heat oil in a medium skillet over medium heat.
- Break eggs into skillet and cook until whites are set and yolks are done as desired.
- Mix together black beans and chili powder in a small bowl.
- Warm the tortillas in the microwave for about 20 seconds to help prevent them from cracking.
- Place equal amounts of beans, green onion, and tomato on the centre of each tortilla. Top each with one egg and sprinkle with shredded cheese.
- Fold in the sides and roll up the wraps.

NUTRIENT	CALORIES	PROTEIN	CARBOHYDRATES	FAT	FIBRE	SODIUM
PER PORTION	419 kcal	27g	40g	18g	10g	253mg

Quick and Easy Breakfast Sandwich

1 PORTION

 **PREP TIME:** 5 minutes |  **TOTAL TIME:** 15 minutes

INGREDIENTS:

- 1 large egg
- ⅛ tsp black pepper
- 2.5 oz (70 g) raw boneless skinless chicken breast, chopped
- 1 oz low fat cheddar cheese, sliced
- 1 tsp (5 mL) canola oil
- 1 large lettuce leaf
- ½ medium tomato, sliced
- 1 thin style whole wheat bun

DIRECTIONS:

- Whisk egg and pepper together in a small bowl; set aside.
- Heat oil in a small non-stick skillet over medium heat.
- Cook chicken for 4-5 minutes, stirring occasionally, until cooked through.
- Move chicken into the centre of the pan and place a small round metal cookie cutter or ring coated lightly in canola oil so it surrounds the chicken.
- Pour egg mixture over chicken and gently stir. Cook for 1 minute or until the egg is almost set and forms a patty shape.
- Place cheese on one half of the bun and microwave on High for 15 seconds or until melted.
- Layer egg mixture, lettuce, and tomato on the bun.

NUTRIENT PER PORTION	CALORIES	PROTEIN	CARBOHYDRATES	FAT	FIBRE	SODIUM
	310 kcal	26g	24g	13g	5g	328mg

Greek-Style Breakfast Wrap

1 PORTION

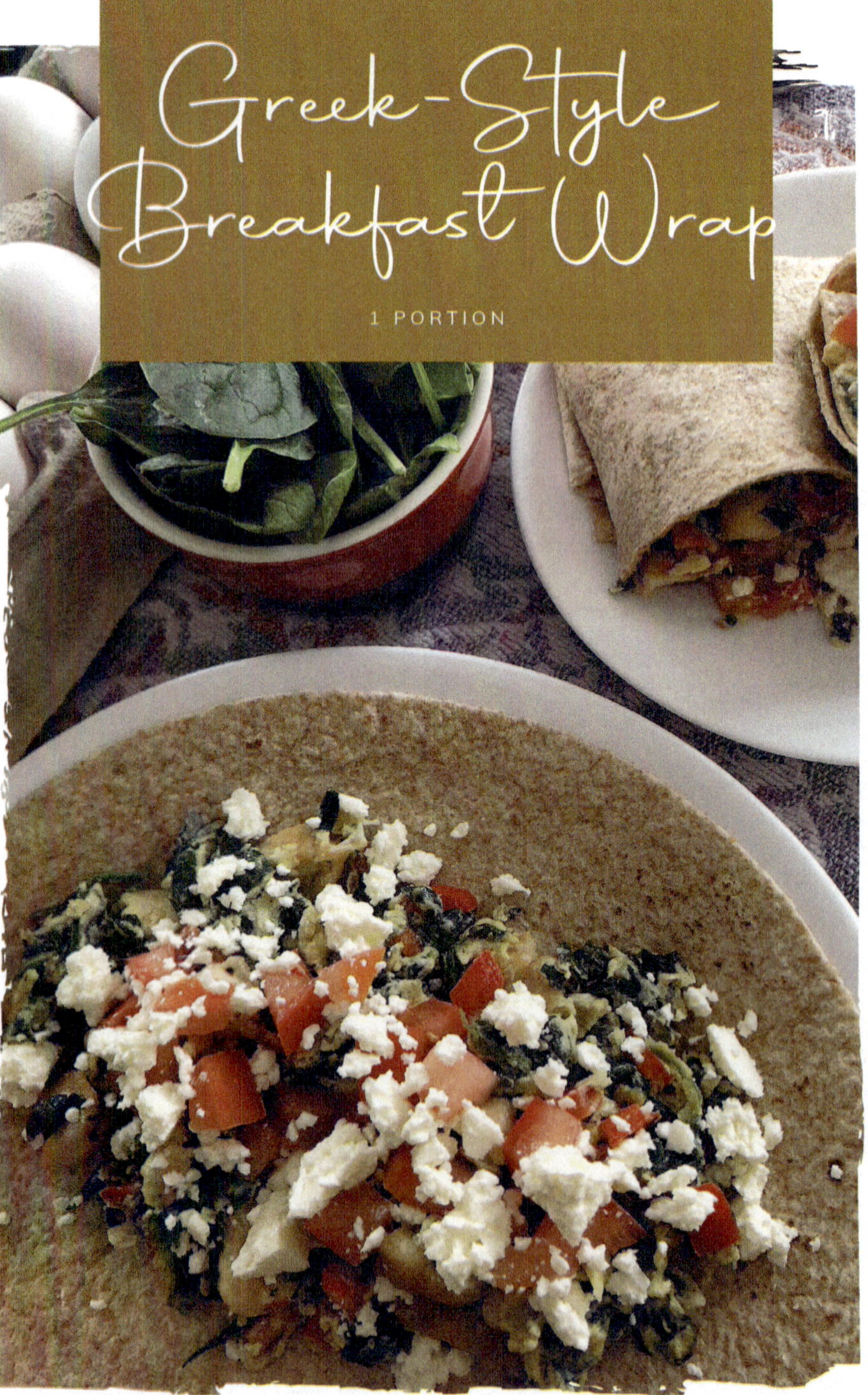

PREP TIME: 5 minutes | **TOTAL TIME:** 20 minutes

INGREDIENTS:

- 1 large egg
- ¼ tsp black pepper
- ⅛ tsp chili powder
- 1 tsp (5 mL) canola oil
- 3 oz (85 g) raw boneless skinless chicken breast, chopped
- 1 garlic clove, minced
- ¼ cup red bell pepper, chopped
- 1 cup fresh spinach, chopped
- 1 8-inch (20 cm) whole wheat flour tortilla
- 1 Tbsp. feta cheese, crumbled
- ¼ cup tomato, chopped

DIRECTIONS:

- Whisk together eggs, pepper, and chili powder; set aside.
- Heat oil in a small non-stick skillet over medium heat.
- Cook chicken for 4-5 minutes, stirring occasionally, until cooked through.
- Add garlic and red bell pepper; cook for 2 minutes more.
- Add spinach; cook for 1-2 minutes or just until wilted.
- Pour egg mixture over vegetables and chicken and gently stir. Cook for 3-4 minutes or until scrambled eggs are fully set.
- Add egg mixture to the center of a tortilla; sprinkle with cheese and chopped tomato.
- Fold in the sides and roll up the wrap.

NUTRIENT PER PORTION	CALORIES	PROTEIN	CARBOHYDRATES	FAT	FIBRE	SODIUM
	364 kcal	28g	27g	17g	5g	554mg

Breakfast in a Mug

1 PORTION

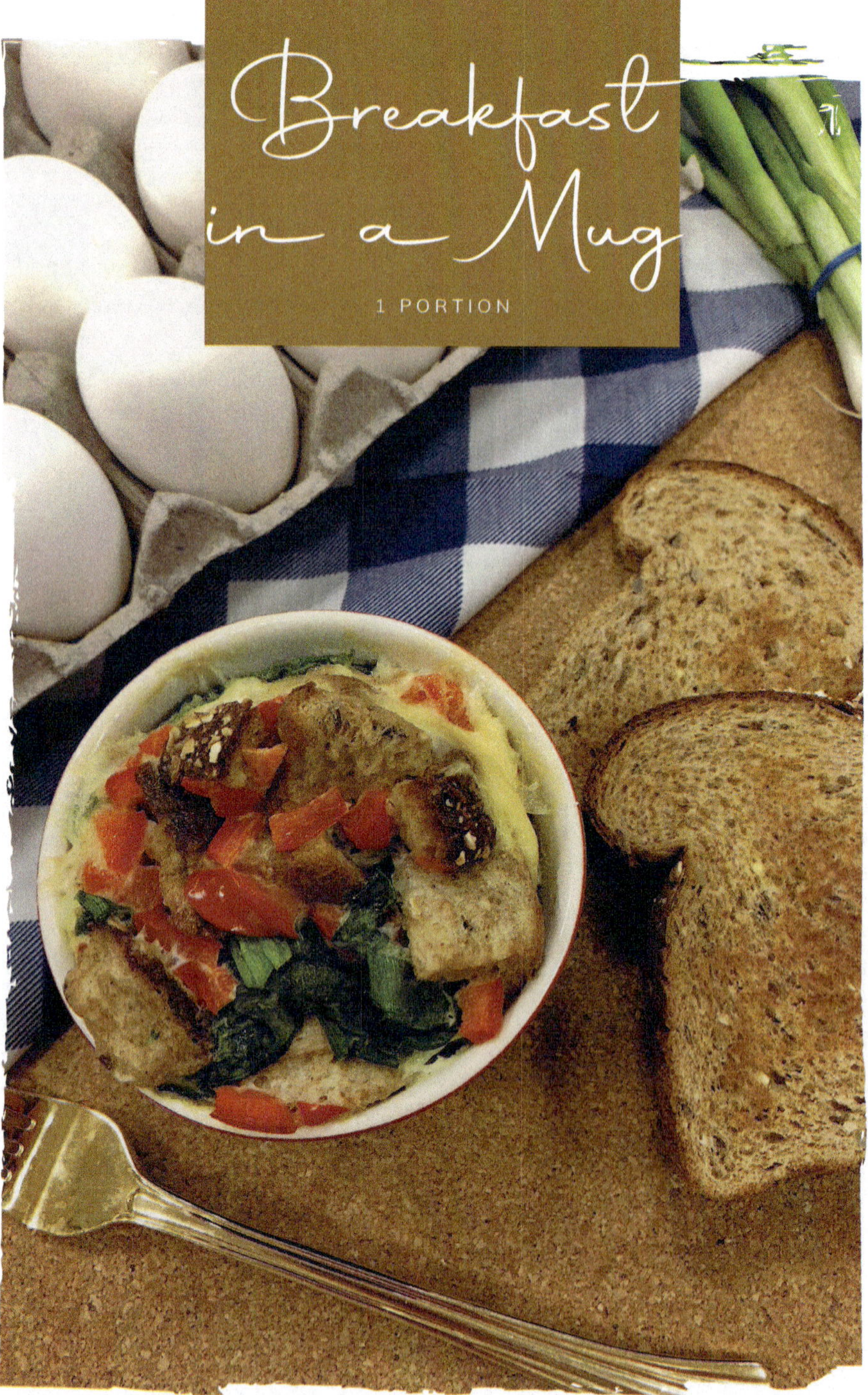

PREP TIME: 5 minutes |  **TOTAL TIME:** 10 minutes

INGREDIENTS:

- 1 tsp (5 mL) canola oil
- 2 oz (57 g) cooked boneless skinless chicken breast, chopped
- 1 slice whole wheat bread, cubed
- 2 Tbsp. red bell pepper, diced
- 2 Tbsp. frozen spinach, thawed and squeezed of excess liquid
- 1 Tbsp. green onion, finely chopped
- 2 large eggs
- 2 Tbsp. (30 mL) 2% milk

DIRECTIONS:

- Spread oil around a microwave-safe mug to coat the inside.
- In the mug, toss chicken with bread, red bell pepper, spinach, and green onion.
- Whisk eggs and milk together in a small bowl; pour over filling.
- Microwave on High for 60 seconds; let stand for 10 seconds. Cook for additional 30-second intervals until the egg is set.

NUTRIENT PER PORTION	CALORIES	PROTEIN	CARBOHYDRATES	FAT	FIBRE	SODIUM
	364 kcal	30g	20g	18g	4g	362mg

Steak and Potato Hash

1 PORTION

 **PREP TIME:** 5 minutes |  **TOTAL TIME:** 35 minutes

INGREDIENTS:

- 1 cup creamer potatoes, quartered
- 2 tsp (10 mL) canola oil, divided
- 4 oz (113 g) raw lean steak
- 1 small onion, chopped
- 1 tsp dried thyme
- 1 garlic clove, minced
- ¼ tsp black pepper
- ¼ tsp paprika
- 4 Brussels sprouts, trimmed and thinly sliced
- 1 tsp (5 mL) white vinegar
- 1 large egg

DIRECTIONS:

- Bring a small pot of water to a boil.
- Add potatoes and boil for 3-5 minutes or until fork tender. Drain potatoes.
- Heat 1 tsp (5 mL) oil in a small skillet over medium heat.
- Cook steak for 5 minutes, flip and cook an additional 5 minutes for a medium rare steak (adjust cooking time as desired). Remove steak from pan and set aside to rest.
- Heat remaining tsp oil in same pan over medium heat.
- Add onion, dried thyme, garlic, black pepper, and paprika; cook, stirring occasionally, for 3-5 minutes or until onions are soft.
- Add Brussels sprouts and 2 Tbsp. (30 mL) of water; cook, stirring occasionally, for 5-7 minutes or until Brussels sprouts start to soften and liquid has evaporated.
- Stir in cooked steak to heat through.
- While the hash is cooking, fill a small pot halfway with water, bring to a boil, and reduce heat to a simmer. Add vinegar.
- Crack egg into an individual cup and slide the egg carefully into the simmering water. Cook until desired firmness, about 3 minutes for a set white and runny yolk.
- Remove egg from the pot with a slotted spoon and set on paper towel to drain excess water.
- Top hash with poached egg.

NUTRIENT PER PORTION	CALORIES	PROTEIN	CARBOHYDRATES	FAT	FIBRE	SODIUM
	412 kcal	30g	40g	15g	9g	73mg

Beef and Pepper Frittata

4 PORTIONS

PREP TIME: 10 minutes | **TOTAL TIME:** 30 minutes

INGREDIENTS:

- 8 large eggs
- ¼ tsp black pepper
- 1 lb (454 g) raw extra lean ground beef
- 1 tsp (5 mL) canola oil
- 1 medium red bell pepper, chopped
- 1 large russet potato, shredded
- 2 garlic cloves, minced
- 1 small onion, chopped
- 1 tsp fennel seeds

DIRECTIONS:

- Preheat broiler to high.
- Whisk eggs, ¼ cup (60 mL) water, and pepper; set aside.
- Cook ground beef in 10-inch (25 cm) ovenproof non-stick skillet over medium heat until no longer pink; drain fat. Remove beef from skillet; set aside.
- Heat oil in the same skillet over medium-high heat.
- Add red bell pepper, potato, garlic and onion; cook, stirring frequently, until soft, approximately 10 minutes.
- Stir in cooked ground beef and fennel seeds.
- Pour egg mixture over filling; lower heat to medium. As mixture sets around edge of skillet, with spatula, gently lift cooked portions to allow uncooked egg to flow underneath. Cook until bottom is set and top is almost set.
- Place skillet under preheated broiler until frittata is puffed and set, 1 to 2 minutes.
- Cut into wedges to serve.

NUTRIENT PER PORTION	CALORIES	PROTEIN	CARBOHYDRATES	FAT	FIBRE	SODIUM
	297 kcal	27g	15g	14g	1g	142mg

Croque Madame Casserole

6 PORTIONS

PREP TIME: 10 minutes | **TOTAL TIME:** 1 hour 20 minutes

INGREDIENTS:

- 1 Tbsp. (15 mL) canola oil
- 10 large eggs
- 1 cup (250 mL) 2% milk
- 2 Tbsp. fresh chives, finely chopped
- 2 garlic cloves, minced
- 1 tsp black pepper
- 8 slices whole wheat bread
- 6 oz (170 g) low sodium lean ham, sliced
- ½ cup Gruyère cheese, shredded
- 3 cups fresh spinach

DIRECTIONS:

- Use oil to grease 13 x 9-inch (3 L) baking dish.
- Whisk together eggs, milk, chives, garlic, and black pepper; pour 1 cup (250 mL) of the egg mixture into baking dish.
- Arrange 4 bread slices on bottom of baking dish.
- Layer half of the ham slices, half of the cheese and half of the spinach over top.
- Repeat layers once.
- Pour remaining egg mixture over top; press gently to allow bread to soak up egg mixture.
- Cover and refrigerate for at least 30 minutes or overnight.
- When ready to bake, preheat oven to 375°F (190°C).
- Bake for 40-45 minutes, or until golden brown and set.

NUTRIENT	CALORIES	PROTEIN	CARBOHYDRATES	FAT	FIBRE	SODIUM
PER PORTION	355 kcal	26g	24g	18g	4g	642mg

Salmon and Ricotta Toast

1 PORTION

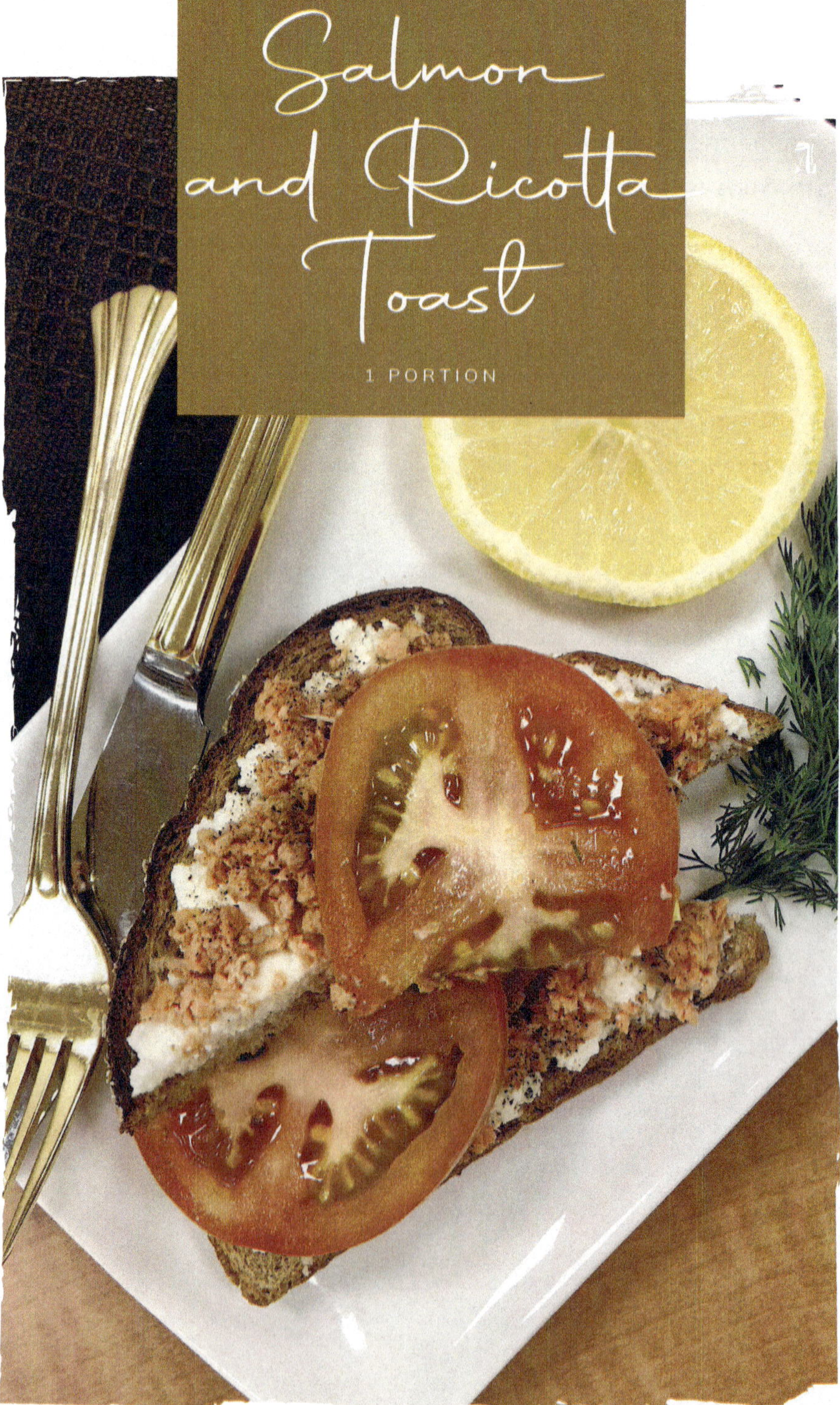

PREP TIME: 5 minutes | **TOTAL TIME:** 5 minutes

INGREDIENTS:

- 1 slice whole wheat bread, toasted
- 3 oz (85 g) canned no sodium added salmon with bones and skin, drained
- 1 Tbsp. (15 mL) lemon juice
- 2 Tbsp. low fat ricotta cheese
- ½ medium tomato, sliced
- ⅛ tsp black pepper

DIRECTIONS:

- Break salmon into flakes and combine with lemon juice.
- Spread ricotta on toast and top with salmon mixture and sliced tomato.
- Sprinkle with black pepper.

NUTRIENT PER PORTION	CALORIES	PROTEIN	CARBOHYDRATES	FAT	FIBRE	SODIUM
	252 kcal	26g	18g	9g	3g	291mg

Cinnamon French Toast

1 PORTION

PREP TIME: 10 minutes | **TOTAL TIME:** 15 minutes

INGREDIENTS:

- 1 large egg
- 2 Tbsp. (30 mL) 2% milk
- 1 slice whole wheat bread
- 1 tsp (5 mL) canola oil
- ¼ tsp cinnamon
- ¾ cup plain 2% Greek yogurt
- ½ cup strawberries, sliced

DIRECTIONS:

- Beat egg with milk in a shallow dish.
- Soak bread slice in egg mixture for 1-2 minutes, flipping bread halfway through.
- Heat oil in small skillet over medium heat.
- Cook soaked bread slice in skillet until browned on both sides, about 2 minutes per side.
- Sprinkle with cinnamon, and top with Greek yogurt and strawberries.

NUTRIENT PER PORTION	CALORIES	PROTEIN	CARBOHYDRATES	FAT	FIBRE	SODIUM
	350 kcal	26g	28g	15g	4g	283mg

High Protein Pancakes

1 PORTION

PREP TIME: 5 minutes | **TOTAL TIME:** 10 minutes

INGREDIENTS:

- ¼ cup 2% cottage cheese
- ¼ cup rolled oats
- 1 large egg
- 1 tsp (5 mL) canola oil
- ½ cup strawberries, sliced
- ½ cup 2% plain Greek yogurt

DIRECTIONS:

- Blend cottage cheese, oats, and egg in a blender until smooth.
- Heat oil in a griddle or small skillet over medium heat.
- Pour about ¼ cup of batter onto griddle for each pancake.
- Cook until browned on both sides and cooked through.
- Top with strawberries and Greek yogurt.

NUTRIENT PER PORTION	CALORIES	PROTEIN	CARBOHYDRATES	FAT	FIBRE	SODIUM
	343 kcal	26g	27g	15g	4g	292mg

Smoothie Bowl

1 PORTION

 **PREP TIME:** 5 minutes |  **TOTAL TIME:** 5 minutes

INGREDIENTS:

- ⅓ cup (80 mL) 2% milk
- ¾ cup plain 2% Greek yogurt
- ½ cup frozen strawberries
- ½ tsp (2.5 mL) vanilla extract
- ½ cup fresh blueberries
- 1 Tbsp. dry roasted sunflower seeds

DIRECTIONS:

- Pour milk into blender, followed by Greek yogurt, frozen strawberries and vanilla.
- Blend until smooth.
- Pour into a bowl; top with blueberries and sunflower seeds.

NUTRIENT PER PORTION	**CALORIES**	**PROTEIN**	**CARBOHYDRATES**	**FAT**	**FIBRE**	**SODIUM**
	260 kcal	18g	29g	9g	4g	90mg

Greek Yogurt Parfait

1 PORTION

PREP TIME: 10 minutes | **TOTAL TIME:** 10 minutes

INGREDIENTS:

- ¼ cup rolled oats
- 1 cup 2% plain Greek yogurt
- ¼ cup (60 mL) 2% milk
- 1 tsp (5 mL) vanilla extract
- 1 tsp ground flaxseed
- ½ cup blueberries

DIRECTIONS:

- Heat a small skillet over medium heat.
- Toast oats, stirring constantly, for 2-3 minutes, or until golden and fragrant.
- Transfer to a bowl and let cool completely.*
- Mix together Greek yogurt, milk, and vanilla extract in a bowl.
- Alternate layers of oats, flaxseed, yogurt, and berries in an individual 1½ cup reusable container or tall glass.

*Note: Toasted oats can be made ahead of time and stored in an airtight container for up to one month.

NUTRIENT PER PORTION	CALORIES	PROTEIN	CARBOHYDRATES	FAT	FIBRE	SODIUM
	322 kcal	25g	37g	8g	5g	105mg

Tropical Overnight Oats

1 PORTION

PREP TIME: 5 minutes | **TOTAL TIME:** 5 minutes

INGREDIENTS:

- ¼ cup rolled oats
- 3 Tbsp. unflavoured whey protein powder
- ½ cup 2% plain Greek yogurt
- ¼ cup (60 mL) 2% milk
- ½ tsp (2.5 mL) vanilla extract
- ½ cup frozen mango chunks
- 1 Tbsp. shredded unsweetened dried coconut

DIRECTIONS:

- Mix oats, protein powder, Greek yogurt, milk, and vanilla extract together in a bowl or container.
- Stir in mango chunks, cover, and place in the fridge overnight.
- When ready to eat, top with shredded coconut.

NUTRIENT PER PORTION	CALORIES	PROTEIN	CARBOHYDRATES	FAT	FIBRE	SODIUM
	337 kcal	26g	39g	9g	4g	98mg

Cinnamon Apple Oatmeal

1 PORTION

PREP TIME: 5 minutes | **TOTAL TIME:** 15 minutes

INGREDIENTS:

- 1 large egg
- ¾ cup (175 mL) 2% milk
- ¼ cup rolled oats
- 3 Tbsp. unflavoured whey protein powder
- 1 small apple, chopped
- ½ tsp cinnamon

DIRECTIONS:

- Beat egg in a bowl, then stir in milk, oats, and protein powder.
- Transfer mixture to saucepan set over medium-low heat.
- Cook, stirring frequently, for 10-12 minutes, or until oats are tender and creamy.
- Top with chopped apple and cinnamon.

NUTRIENT	CALORIES	PROTEIN	CARBOHYDRATES	FAT	FIBRE	SODIUM
PER PORTION	351 kcal	27g	38g	11g	5g	183mg

Lunch
RECIPES

Tortilla Pizza

1 PORTION

PREP TIME: 10 minutes | **TOTAL TIME:** 25 minutes

INGREDIENTS:

- 2 oz (57 g) cooked extra-lean ground beef
- 1 8-inch (20 cm) whole wheat flour tortilla
- ¼ cup (60 mL) no sodium added tomato sauce
- ½ tsp dried oregano
- ½ cup fresh spinach
- 2 medium button mushrooms, sliced
- 1/2 medium red bell pepper, sliced
- ½ small onion, diced
- ¼ cup low fat mozzarella cheese, shredded

DIRECTIONS:

- Preheat oven to 400°F (200°C).
- Place tortilla on a baking sheet.
- Spread tomato sauce evenly over tortilla; sprinkle with dried oregano.
- Lay spinach over the tortilla.
- Add ground beef, mushrooms, bell pepper and onion.
- Top with mozzarella cheese.
- Bake in oven for 10 minutes, or until cheese is melted and edges are crispy.

NUTRIENT PER PORTION	CALORIES	PROTEIN	CARBOHYDRATES	FAT	FIBRE	SODIUM
	467 kcal	36g	47g	16g	8g	608mg

Salmon Tostada

1 PORTION

 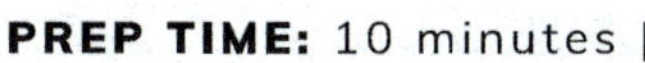 

PREP TIME: 10 minutes | **TOTAL TIME:** 20 minutes

INGREDIENTS:

- 1 tsp chili powder
- ½ tsp ground cumin
- 1 Tbsp. (30 mL) lime juice
- 4 oz (113 g) fresh or frozen and thawed salmon fillet
- 2 5-inch (13 cm) soft corn tortillas
- 2 Tbsp. fresh cilantro, chopped
- 1 medium tomato, chopped
- 2 Tbsp. red onion, sliced

COLESLAW:

- ½ cup savoy cabbage, shredded
- ¼ cup plain 2% Greek yogurt
- 1 Tbsp. (30 mL) lime juice

DIRECTIONS:

- Preheat oven to 400°F (200°C). Line a baking sheet with parchment paper.
- Mix together chili powder, cumin, and lime juice in a bowl.
- Spread over salmon and place salmon on baking sheet.
- Cook for 8-10 minutes or until fish flakes easily with a fork.
- Mix together cabbage, Greek yogurt, and lime juice in a bowl.
- Warm the tortillas in the microwave for about 20 seconds to help prevent them from cracking.
- Flake salmon and place half onto each corn tortilla.
- Top each with half of the coleslaw mix.
- Divide cilantro, tomato, and red onion between the two tostadas.

NUTRIENT PER PORTION	CALORIES	PROTEIN	CARBOHYDRATES	FAT	FIBRE	SODIUM
	328 kcal	26g	27g	14g	6g	127mg

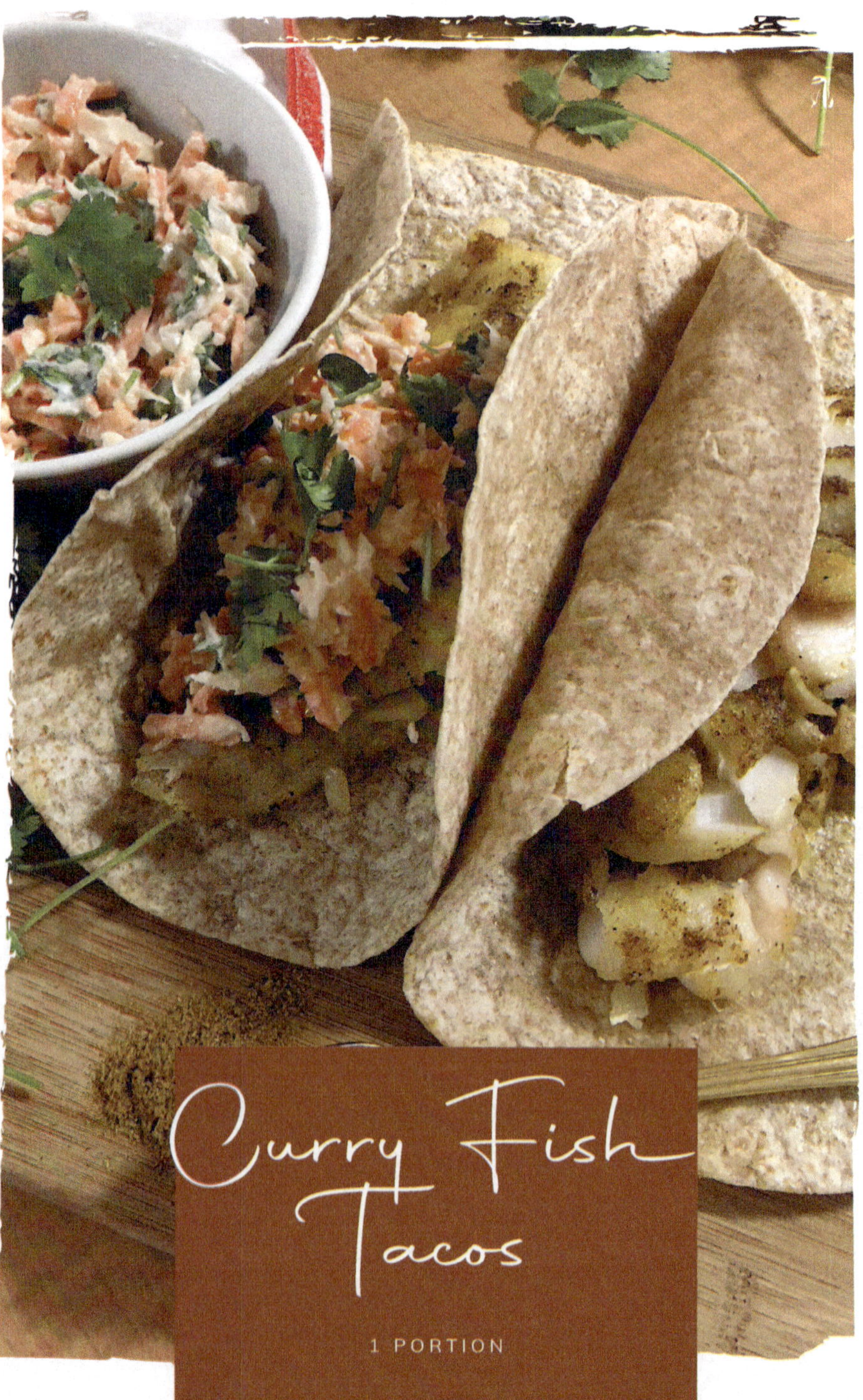

Curry Fish Tacos

1 PORTION

PREP TIME: 10 minutes |  **TOTAL TIME:** 20 minutes

INGREDIENTS:

- 1 tsp (5 mL) canola oil
- 4 oz (113 g) fresh or frozen and thawed cod fillet
- ½ tsp curry powder
- ⅛ tsp black pepper
- 2 5-inch (13 cm) soft corn or whole wheat tortillas*

COLESLAW:

- 1 cup savoy cabbage, shredded
- 1 small carrot, shredded
- 2 Tbsp. fresh cilantro, chopped
- ¼ cup plain 2% Greek yogurt
- 1 Tbsp. (15 mL) lime juice

DIRECTIONS:

- Heat oil in a small skillet over medium high heat.
- Season one side of cod with half of the curry powder and black pepper.
- Place seasoned side down in skillet.
- Sprinkle remaining seasoning on the other side of cod.
- Cook until golden brown on both sides and cooked through, approximately 3-4 minutes per side, or until it flakes easily with a fork. Remove cod from pan onto a plate; set aside.
- Mix together cabbage, carrot, cilantro, Greek yogurt, and lime juice in a bowl.
- Place half a piece of fish onto each corn tortilla.
- Top with coleslaw.

*Note: Nutrient analysis done with corn tortillas.

NUTRIENT PER PORTION	CALORIES	PROTEIN	CARBOHYDRATES	FAT	FIBRE	SODIUM
	275 kcal	29g	25g	8g	6g	148mg

Philly Cheesesteak Sandwich

1 PORTION

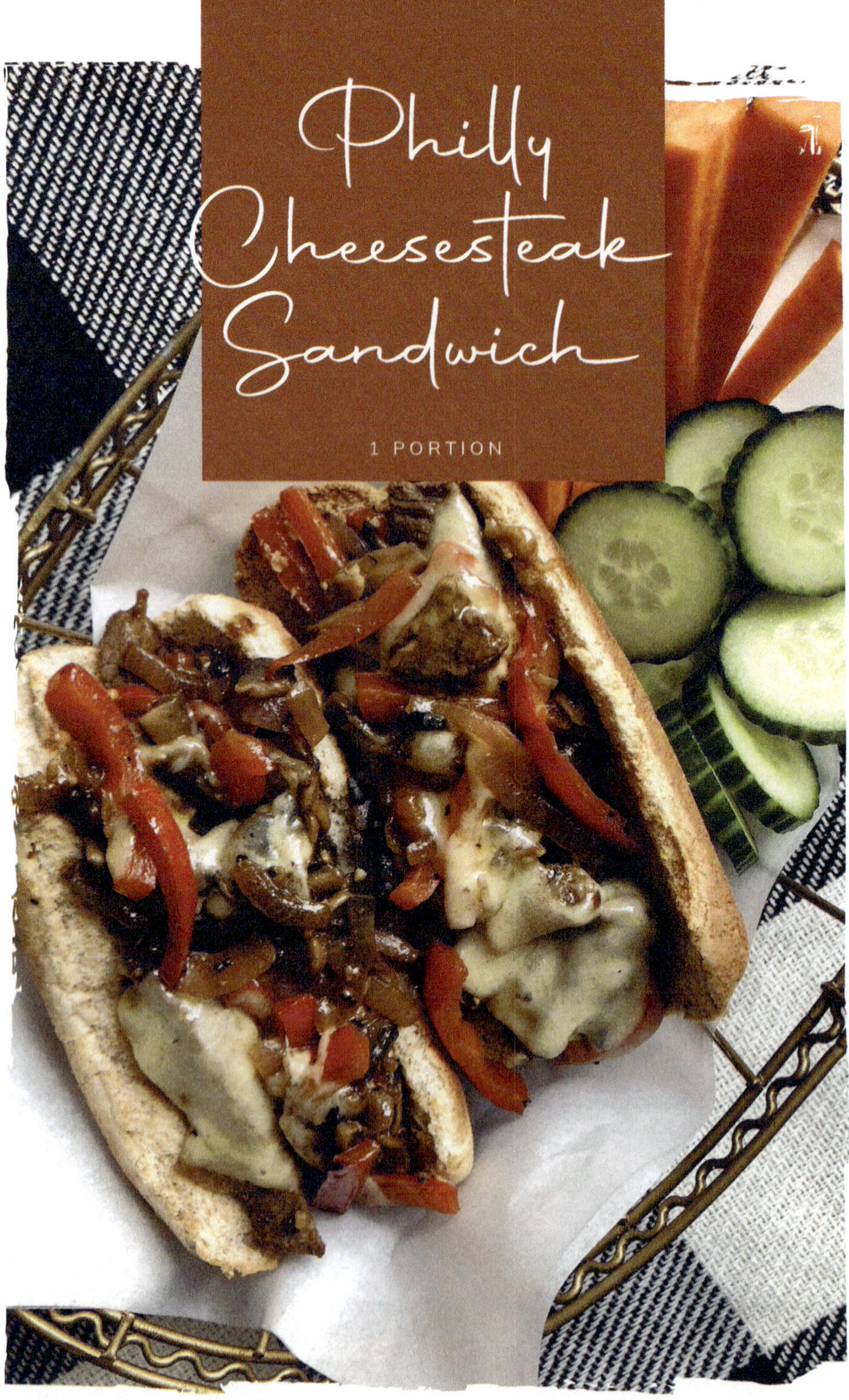

PREP TIME: 15 minutes |  TOTAL TIME: 30 minutes

INGREDIENTS:

- 3 oz (85 g) raw lean steak
- ½ small onion, thinly sliced
- 4 medium button mushrooms, thinly sliced
- 1 medium red bell pepper, thinly sliced
- 1 tsp (5 mL) canola oil
- ¼ tsp black pepper
- 1 slice provolone cheese
- 1 whole wheat hot dog bun

DIRECTIONS:

- Place steak in freezer for 15 minutes to firm up so it is easier to slice.
- Heat 2 Tbsp. water in a medium skillet over medium high heat.
- Add onion and cook until translucent, approximately 3 minutes. Add mushrooms and peppers and cook until tender, approximately 5 minutes. Remove vegetables from pan and set aside.
- Remove the meat from the freezer and slice very thinly against the grain.
- Heat oil in the same skillet over medium heat.
- Add steak slices, season with black pepper and cook over medium heat until desired doneness, about 1 minute per side.
- Turn heat off, add vegetables back to the pan and top with a slice of provolone cheese.
- Add a small splash of water and cover the skillet with a lid to melt the cheese.
- Transfer filling onto the bun.

NUTRIENT PER PORTION	CALORIES	PROTEIN	CARBOHYDRATES	FAT	FIBRE	SODIUM
	424 kcal	34g	36g	17g	6g	530 mg

Chicken Lettuce Wraps

1 PORTION

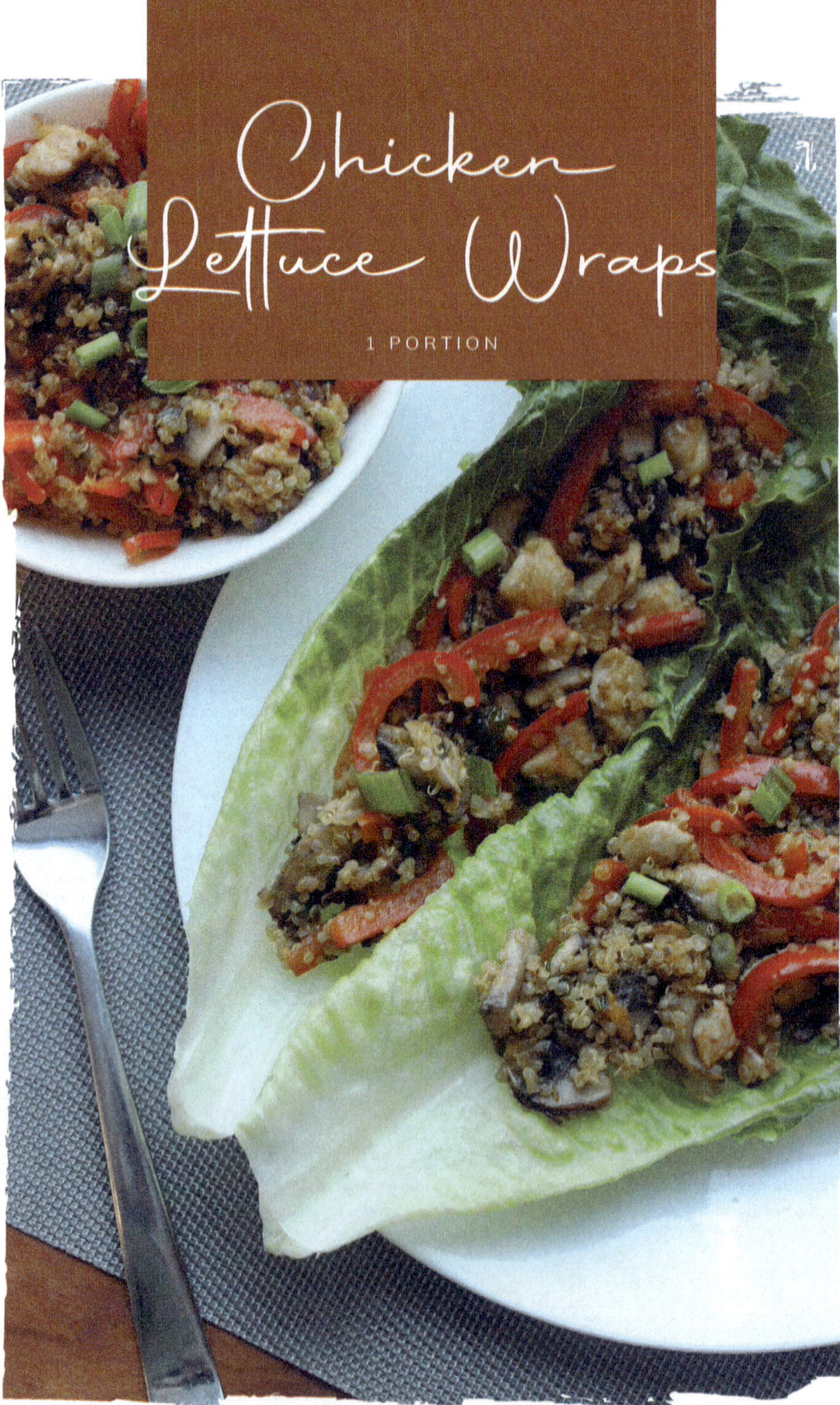

PREP TIME: 5 minutes | **TOTAL TIME:** 15 minutes

INGREDIENTS:

- 1 tsp (5 mL) canola oil
- 5 oz (142 g) raw boneless skinless chicken breast, chopped
- 1 garlic clove, grated
- 1 tsp ginger, grated
- 2 medium green onions, sliced
- 4 medium button mushrooms, thinly sliced
- 1 small red bell pepper, thinly sliced
- ½ cup quinoa, cooked
- 1 tsp (5 mL) low sodium soy sauce
- 2 tsp (10 mL) unseasoned rice wine vinegar
- 2 large romaine leaves

DIRECTIONS:

- Heat oil in a medium skillet over medium high heat.
- Cook chicken for 4-5 minutes, stirring occasionally, until cooked through.
- Add garlic, ginger, green onion, mushroom, and red bell pepper; cook 3-4 minutes until vegetables just begin to soften.
- Mix in quinoa, soy sauce, and rice wine vinegar until heated through.
- Divide filling between the two romaine leaves.

NUTRIENT	CALORIES	PROTEIN	CARBOHYDRATES	FAT	FIBRE	SODIUM
PER PORTION	302 kcal	30g	28g	8g	6g	273mg

Chicken Shawarma Pita

2 PORTIONS

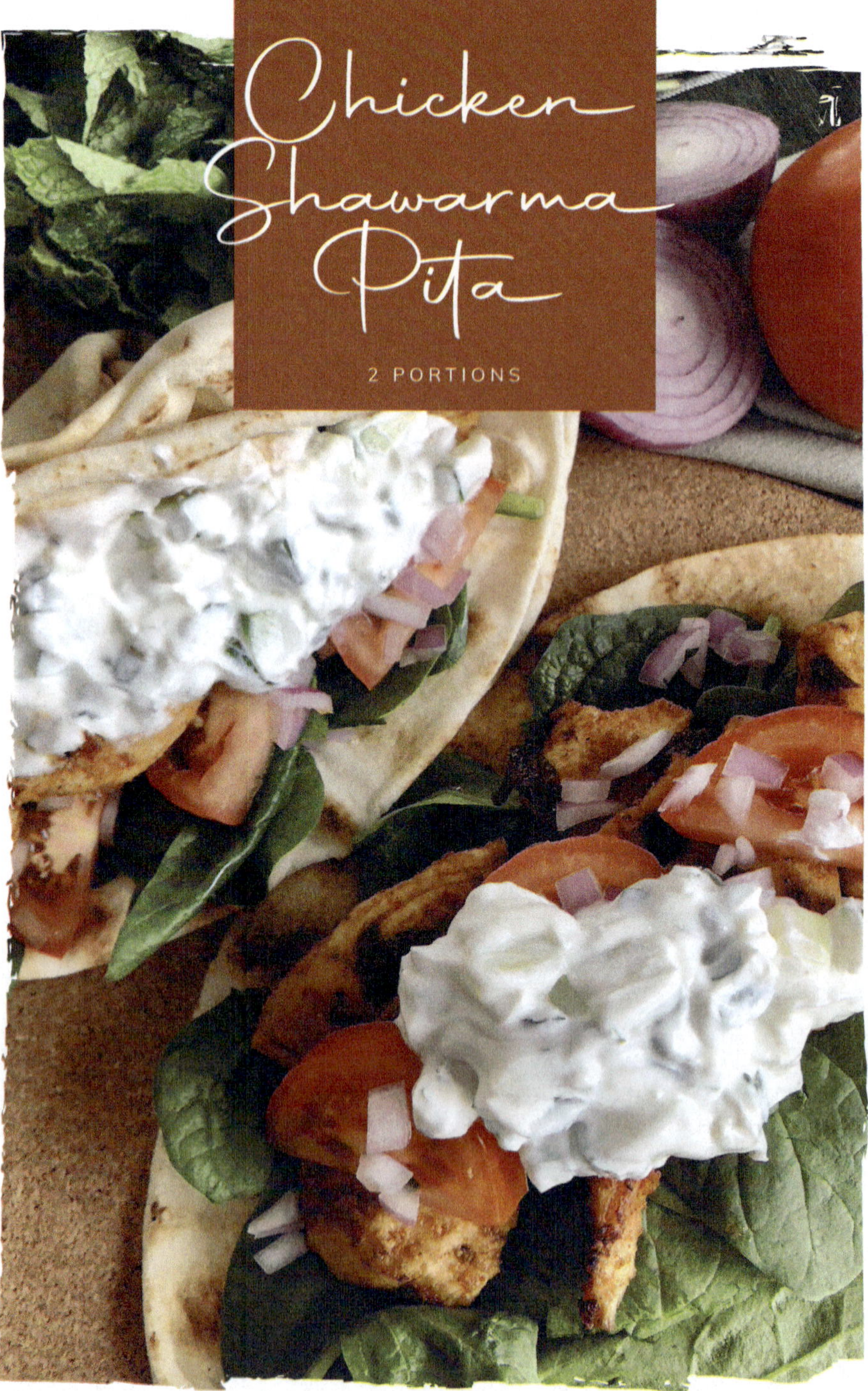

PREP TIME: 35 minutes | **TOTAL TIME:** 45 minutes

INGREDIENTS:

- 1 garlic clove, minced
- ½ tsp black pepper
- 1 tsp cayenne pepper
- 1 Tbsp. ground coriander
- 1 Tbsp. ground cumin
- 2 tsp paprika
- 2 Tbsp. (30 mL) lemon juice
- 1 Tbsp. (15 mL) olive oil
- ½ cup fresh mint, chopped
- 6 oz (170 g) raw boneless skinless chicken breast, sliced into thin strips
- 1 tsp (5 mL) canola oil
- 1 small whole wheat pita with a pocket, cut in half
- 2 Tbsp. red onion, finely chopped
- 2 cups fresh spinach
- 1 medium tomato, chopped

YOGURT DRESSING:

- 1 cup plain 2% Greek yogurt
- ½ cup cucumber, chopped
- 2 Tbsp. fresh mint, chopped
- 2 Tbsp. lemon juice
- 1 garlic clove, minced

DIRECTIONS:

- Combine minced garlic, black pepper, cayenne pepper, coriander, cumin, paprika, lemon juice, olive oil, and mint in a medium bowl.
- Add chicken and mix with marinade; cover with plastic wrap and refrigerate chicken and allow to marinate for at least 30 minutes and up to overnight.
- Heat canola oil in a medium skillet over medium high heat.
- Add marinated chicken and cook, stirring occasionally, until fully cooked through, approximately 8-10 minutes.
- In a small bowl stir together ingredients for yogurt dressing.
- Slice open pita and stuff each half with chicken, red onion, spinach, and tomatoes.
- Top with yogurt dressing.

NUTRIENT PER PORTION	CALORIES	PROTEIN	CARBOHYDRATES	FAT	FIBRE	SODIUM
	375 kcal	31g	34g	8g	4g	253mg

Bánh Mì

4 PORTIONS

PREP TIME: 45 minutes | **TOTAL TIME:** 1 hour 15 minutes

INGREDIENTS:

- 2 medium carrots, thinly sliced into matchsticks
- 1 cucumber, thinly sliced into matchsticks
- 4 small radishes, thinly sliced
- ¼ cup (60 mL) unseasoned rice wine vinegar
- 1 lb (454 g) raw pork tenderloin, trimmed of silver skin
- 1 cup fresh cilantro, chopped
- 1 jalapeño, thinly sliced
- 1 whole wheat baguette

YOGURT DRESSING:

- ½ cup plain 2% Greek yogurt
- 1 tsp (5 mL) low sodium soy sauce

DIRECTIONS:

- Preheat oven to 400°F (200°C). Line a baking sheet with parchment paper.
- Toss carrot, cucumber and radish with rice wine vinegar in a large bowl.
- Cover and refrigerate for at least 30 minutes.
- Place tenderloin on baking sheet and roast in the oven for 25-30 minutes, flipping halfway through. Let the tenderloin rest for at least 10 minutes before slicing.
- Drain vegetables when ready to use.
- Mix together yogurt dressing ingredients in a small bowl.
- Split baguette in half lengthwise and spread evenly with yogurt sauce.
- Layer with cilantro, jalapeño, pickled vegetables, and cooked pork.
- Cut baguette into quarters.

NUTRIENT PER PORTION	CALORIES	PROTEIN	CARBOHYDRATES	FAT	FIBRE	SODIUM
	298 kcal	33g	33g	3g	3g	407mg

Shrimp Noodle Salad

1 PORTION

PREP TIME: 10 minutes |  TOTAL TIME: 30 minutes

INGREDIENTS:

- 2 oz (57 g) dried soba or buckwheat noodles
- 1 tsp (5 mL) canola oil
- 12 medium peeled and deveined shrimp, frozen and thawed or fresh
- 2 cups savoy cabbage, shredded
- 1 medium carrot, shredded
- 1 green onion, thinly sliced
- ½ fresh Thai red chili, thinly sliced
- 1 tsp (5 mL) sesame oil
- 2 Tbsp. (30 mL) unseasoned rice wine vinegar

DIRECTIONS:

- Cook noodles according to package directions; drain using a colander and pour noodles into a large bowl of cold water.
- Rub the noodles between your hands to remove excess starch.
- Drain the cold water, rinse the noodles again and return noodles to the bowl; set aside.
- Heat canola oil in a small skillet over medium high heat.
- Add shrimp; cook for 2-3 minutes per side or until shrimp is pink and cooked through. Remove shrimp from pan onto a plate; set aside.
- Combine cabbage, carrot, green onion, Thai red chilies, sesame oil, and rice wine vinegar.
- Mix in cooked noodles and shrimp.

NUTRIENT PER PORTION	CALORIES	PROTEIN	CARBOHYDRATES	FAT	FIBRE	SODIUM
	335 kcal	25g	37g	11g	6g	433mg

Grilled Surf and Turf Salad

1 PORTION

PREP TIME: 10 minutes | **TOTAL TIME:** 15 minutes

INGREDIENTS:

- 3 wooden or metal skewers
- 1 tsp (5 mL) canola oil
- 1 Tbsp. (15 mL) lemon juice
- ¼ tsp chili powder
- ¼ tsp black pepper
- 8 medium peeled and deveined shrimp, frozen and thawed or fresh
- 2 oz (57 g) raw sirloin steak, cut into 1 inch (2.5 cm) cubes
- ½ cup brown rice, cooked
- 2 cups fresh spinach
- ¼ cucumber, chopped
- 1 medium tomato, chopped
- 2 Tbsp. red onion, chopped
- 2 Tbsp. feta cheese, crumbled
- 1 Tbsp. (15 mL) balsamic vinegar

DIRECTIONS:

- If using, place wooden skewers in a bowl of cold water to soak.
- Brush grill or grill pan lightly with oil and preheat to medium heat.
- Mix together lemon juice, chili powder, and black pepper in a bowl.
- Add shrimp and toss to coat shrimp.
- Remove wooden skewers from water or take metal skewers and thread four shrimp onto two skewers and the steak onto the third.
- Grill skewers for 2-3 minutes per side or until shrimp is pink and cooked through, and steak is done as desired.
- Add rice to the serving dish, and top with spinach.
- Sprinkle on cucumber, tomato, red onion, and feta cheese.
- Remove shrimp and steak from skewers and add to salad.
- Drizzle with balsamic vinegar.

NUTRIENT PER PORTION	CALORIES	PROTEIN	CARBOHYDRATES	FAT	FIBRE	SODIUM
	410 kcal	32g	40g	14g	6g	387mg

Taco Salad

1 PORTION

PREP TIME: 10 minutes | 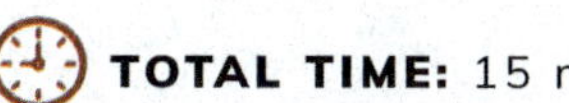 **TOTAL TIME:** 15 minutes

INGREDIENTS:

- 2.5 oz (70 g) cooked extra-lean ground beef
- 1 tsp chili powder
- ½ tsp ground cumin
- ½ cup cooked brown rice
- 4 lettuce leaves, chopped
- 1 medium tomato, chopped
- 2 Tbsp. fresh cilantro, chopped
- ½ cup frozen corn kernels, thawed
- 1 medium green onion, chopped
- 2 Tbsp. low fat cheddar cheese, shredded
- 2 Tbsp. plain 2% Greek yogurt
- 1 Tbsp. (15 mL) lime juice

DIRECTIONS:

- Mix ground beef, chili powder and cumin together.
- Add the rice to serving dish, top with lettuce.
- Sprinkle on seasoned ground beef, tomato, cilantro, corn, green onion, and cheese.
- Top with Greek yogurt and lime juice.

NUTRIENT PER PORTION	CALORIES	PROTEIN	CARBOHYDRATES	FAT	FIBRE	SODIUM
	438 kcal	34g	57g	10g	10g	254 mg

Tuna Black Bean Salad

CONTRIBUTED BY: JENNIFER BLACK, RD

3 PORTIONS

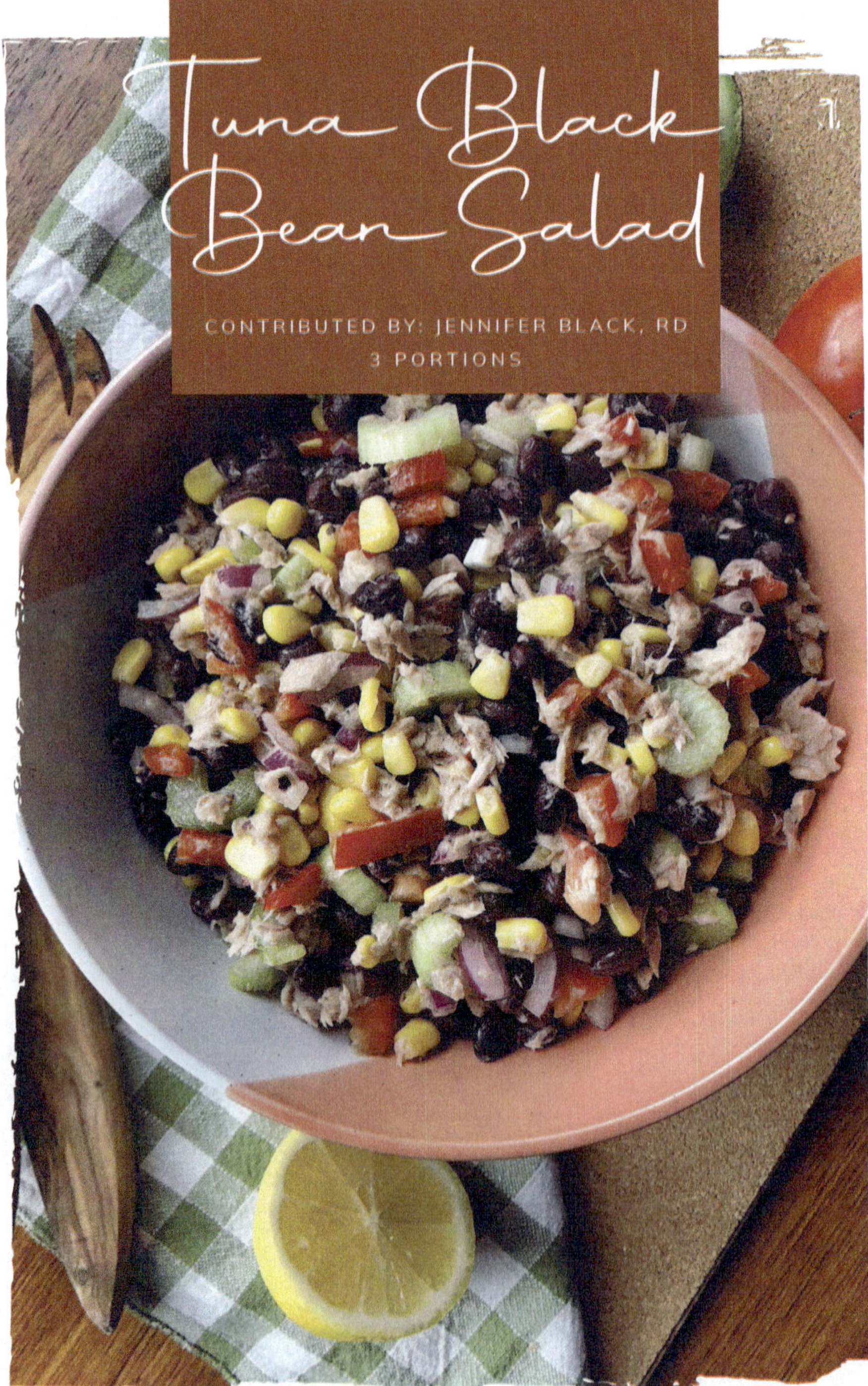

PREP TIME: 10 minutes | **TOTAL TIME:** 10 minutes

INGREDIENTS:

- 1 can (120 g) low sodium tuna, drained
- 1 can (14 oz/398 mL) no sodium added black beans, drained and rinsed
- 1 celery stalk, diced
- 1 cup frozen corn kernels, thawed
- ¼ small onion, diced
- 1 small red bell pepper, chopped

DRESSING:

- 2 Tbsp. (30 mL) olive oil
- ¼ tsp black pepper
- 2 Tbsp. (30 mL) lemon juice

DIRECTIONS:

- Mix together tuna, black beans, celery, corn, onion, and red bell pepper in a large bowl.
- Mix dressing ingredients together and pour over tuna mixture.
- Toss salad.

NUTRIENT PER PORTION	CALORIES	PROTEIN	CARBOHYDRATES	FAT	FIBRE	SODIUM
	351 kcal	25g	41g	11g	9g	46mg

Egg Drop Soup

1 PORTION

PREP TIME: 5 minutes | **TOTAL TIME:** 30 minutes

INGREDIENTS:

- 2 cups (500 mL) no sodium added chicken broth
- ½-inch (1 cm) piece ginger, cut into rounds
- 2.5 oz (70 g) raw boneless skinless chicken breast, chopped
- 4 medium button mushrooms, thinly sliced
- 2 baby bok choy, thinly sliced
- 1 tsp cornstarch
- 1 large egg, beaten
- ½ cup brown rice, cooked

DIRECTIONS:

- Heat broth in a saucepan and over medium-high heat with ginger rounds and chopped chicken.
- Simmer for 15 minutes and remove ginger with a slotted spoon.
- Add sliced mushroom and bok choy to broth and cook for 5 minutes, or until chicken is fully cooked.
- Mix cornstarch and 2 Tbsp. of hot broth in a small bowl until corn starch is fully dissolved.
- Slowly pour in the cornstarch mixture while stirring the soup for 2-3 minutes to slightly thicken soup. Reduce heat to a simmer.
- Pour in the egg slowly while gently stirring the soup.
- Turn off the heat and let the soup stand for 30 seconds to finish cooking the wispy egg.
- Place brown rice and green onion in a bowl and ladle in soup.

NUTRIENT	CALORIES	PROTEIN	CARBOHYDRATES	FAT	FIBRE	SODIUM
PER PORTION	288 kcal	23g	33g	7g	4g	144mg

Beef Pho

4 PORTIONS

PREP TIME: 20 minutes | **TOTAL TIME:** 50 minutes

INGREDIENTS:

- 4 dried shiitake mushrooms
- ½ lb (227 g) raw flank steak, trimmed of fat
- 6 cups (1.4 L) no sodium added beef broth
- 4-inch (10 cm) piece ginger, cut into rounds
- 1 cinnamon stick
- 2 star anise
- 1 Tbsp. (15 mL) lime juice
- 4 oz dried rice noodles
- 4 large eggs
- 4 cups savoy cabbage, shredded
- 2 cups bean sprouts
- 4 medium green onions, thinly sliced
- 2 fresh Thai red chilies, thinly sliced
- 8 fresh basil leaves

DIRECTIONS:

- Reconstitute dried mushrooms in ½ cup of warm water for 15 minutes.
- Place beef in freezer for 15 minutes to firm up so it is easier to slice.
- Combine beef broth, ginger, cinnamon, and star anise in a medium saucepan over high heat and bring to a boil.
- Reduce heat to medium and simmer for 5 minutes. Stir in lime juice and continue to simmer.
- Cook noodles in a medium pot of boiling water according to package directions. Drain well and set noodles aside.
- Refill pot with water; bring to a boil and add the eggs still in the shell. Turn off the heat and let cook for 7 minutes for a just set yolk.
- Remove mushrooms from water and discard stems.
- Slice mushroom caps and place one cap into each bowl.
- Ladle mushroom broth into soup broth, leaving out any sediment that may have settled on the bottom. Discard remaining mushroom broth.
- Remove beef from freezer and slice as thinly as possible against the grain.
- Add to simmering broth and cook for about 8 minutes or as desired.
- Remove ginger, cinnamon, and star anise from broth.
- Divide noodles equally among the four bowls and top with cabbage.
- Ladle broth and beef into bowls.
- Garnish with bean sprouts, green onion, Thai red chili and basil.
- Carefully peel the eggs and slice in half lengthwise. Add one egg to each bowl.

NUTRIENT	CALORIES	PROTEIN	CARBOHYDRATES	FAT	FIBRE	SODIUM
PER PORTION	361 kcal	26g	37g	12g	4g	181mg

Classic Beef Stew

6 PORTIONS

PREP TIME: 20 minutes | **TOTAL TIME:** 2 hours

INGREDIENTS:

- 2 tsp (10 mL) canola oil, divided
- 1 lb (454 g) raw beef eye of round stew meat, cubed
- 1 large onion, chopped
- 2 Tbsp. (30 mL) tomato paste
- 1 cup (250 mL) dry red wine*
- 2 garlic cloves, minced
- 2 bay leaves
- 1 tsp black pepper
- 2 tsp fresh thyme
- 3 cups (750 mL) no sodium added beef broth
- 3 medium carrots, chopped
- 3 celery stalks, chopped
- 2 large russet potatoes, chopped
- 1 cup frozen peas

DIRECTIONS:

- Heat 1 tsp oil in a large dutch oven or stock pot over medium high heat.
- Brown the meat in batches, approximately 2-3 minutes per side. Remove beef from pot; set aside.
- Heat remaining tsp of oil in the same pot over medium heat.
- Add onions and cook until they begin to soften, approximately 5 minutes.
- Add tomato paste and stir until fragrant. Deglaze with 1 cup red wine and scrape the browned bits of the bottom of the pot.
- Stir in garlic, bay leaves, black pepper, thyme and return beef to pot.
- Add beef broth, and add additional water if necessary to cover the beef completely.
- Bring to a simmer and cook covered until beef is almost tender, about 1 hour.
- Add carrots, celery and potato; cook stew covered until meat and vegetables are tender, about 30 minutes.
- Stir in frozen peas during the last 5 minutes of cooking.

*Note: May substitute red wine with no sodium added beef broth, if desired.

NUTRIENT PER PORTION	CALORIES	PROTEIN	CARBOHYDRATES	FAT	FIBRE	SODIUM
	293 kcal	22g	35g	4g	5g	106mg

Salmon Cakes

2 PORTIONS

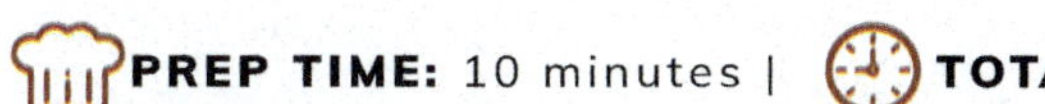

PREP TIME: 10 minutes | **TOTAL TIME:** 30 minutes

INGREDIENTS:

- 1 tsp (5 mL) canola oil
- 6 oz (170 g) can no sodium added salmon with bones and skin, drained
- 1 large egg
- 1 medium green onion, finely chopped
- ¼ cup red bell pepper, finely chopped
- ¼ cup fine whole wheat bread crumbs
- ½ tsp black pepper
- ¼ cup fresh dill, chopped
- 2 Tbsp. (30 mL) lemon juice

YOGURT DRESSING:

- 2 Tbsp. fresh dill, chopped
- 1 Tbsp. (15 mL) lemon juice
- ¼ cup plain 2% Greek yogurt

SIDES:

- ½ cup quinoa, uncooked
- 2 cups broccoli florets

DIRECTIONS:

- Preheat oven to 400°F (200°C).
- Cook quinoa according to package directions.
- Line a baking sheet with foil and brush lightly with oil.
- Mash salmon with a fork to mix the fish with the bones and skin.
- Add remaining salmon cakes ingredients (egg, green onion, red bell pepper, bread crumbs, black pepper, dill, and lemon juice) and mix well.
- Divide mixture into quarters and shape each into a patty.
- Place on a baking sheet and bake for 10 minutes, flipping halfway through.
- While salmon cakes bake, steam broccoli florets for 8-10 minutes or until tender.
- Combine yogurt dressing ingredients in a small bowl and set aside.
- Divide cooked quinoa and steamed broccoli between 2 plates.
- Place 2 patties on each plate and spoon on yogurt dressing.

NUTRIENT	CALORIES	PROTEIN	CARBOHYDRATES	FAT	FIBRE	SODIUM
PER PORTION	360 kcal	28g	32g	13g	5g	240mg

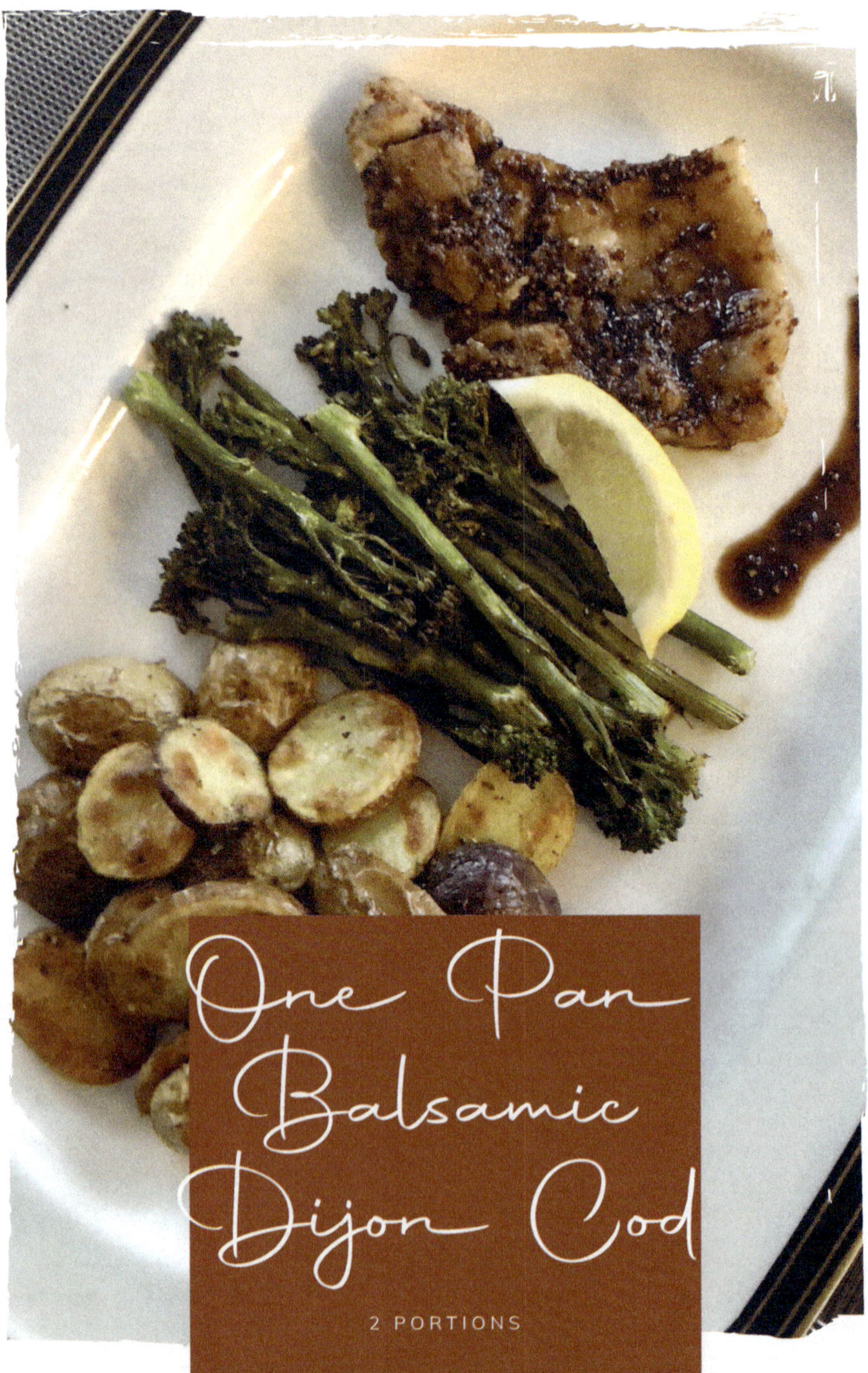

One Pan Balsamic Dijon Cod

2 PORTIONS

PREP TIME: 10 minutes | **TOTAL TIME:** 40 minutes

INGREDIENTS:

- 2 cups creamer potatoes, halved
- 2 tsp (10 mL) canola oil
- 2 tsp dried oregano
- ½ tsp black pepper
- 2 Tbsp. (30 mL) balsamic vinegar
- 2 tsp (10 mL) Dijon mustard
- 2 cups broccoli florets, chopped
- 2 - 5 oz (142 g) fresh or frozen and thawed cod fillets

DIRECTIONS:

- Preheat oven to 400°F (200°C). Line a baking sheet with foil.
- Toss potatoes with oil and oregano. Spread potatoes on baking sheet and bake for 10 minutes.
- Stir together black pepper, balsamic vinegar, and Dijon mustard in a small bowl to make a glaze; set aside.
- Add broccoli to the baking sheet, flip the potatoes and bake for 10 minutes more.
- Take the baking sheet out of the oven and add the cod. Cook for 5 minutes more then remove baking sheet from oven.
- Flip the broccoli and brush cod with the glaze.
- Bake for another 5 minutes or until fish flakes easily with a fork and broccoli is tender.
- Divide potatoes, broccoli and fish between 2 dishes.

NUTRIENT PER PORTION	CALORIES	PROTEIN	CARBOHYDRATES	FAT	FIBRE	SODIUM
	309 kcal	30g	35g	6g	7g	230mg

Tex-Mex Stuffed Peppers

4 PORTIONS

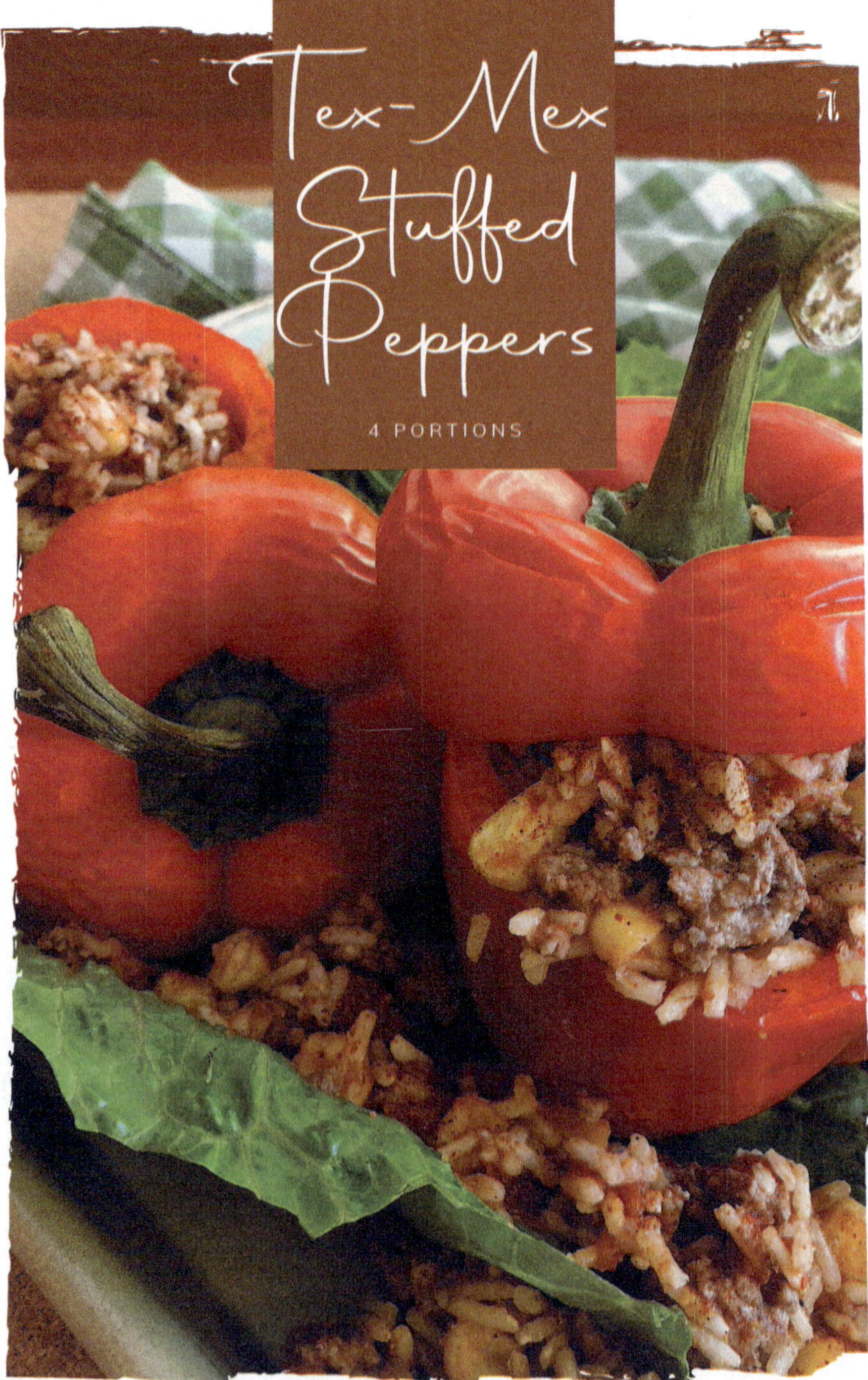

PREP TIME: 40 minutes | **TOTAL TIME:** 1 hour

INGREDIENTS:

- ¾ cup brown rice, uncooked
- 1 tsp (5 mL) canola oil
- ¾ lb (341 g) raw extra lean ground beef
- 4 medium bell peppers
- 1 can (14 oz/398 mL) no sodium added diced tomatoes
- ½ cup frozen corn kernels, thawed
- 1 Tbsp. chili powder
- 1 Tbsp. ground cumin
- ¼ cup cilantro, chopped

DIRECTIONS:

- Preheat oven to 400°F (200°C).
- Cook rice according to package directions.
- Heat oil in a large skillet on medium heat.
- Add ground beef and cook until no longer pink; drain fat. Remove beef from skillet; set aside.
- Cut tops off peppers; remove and discard membranes and seeds inside the peppers.
- Spoon approximately ½ cup of diced tomatoes on the bottom of an 8 x 8-inch (1.4 L) baking dish and stand peppers in the dish. Cover the dish with foil and bake for 10 minutes to slightly soften peppers.
- Mix cooked ground beef, corn, brown rice, chili powder, cumin, and remaining diced tomatoes in a large bowl.
- Spoon filling into peppers.
- Bake 20 minutes uncovered or until peppers are tender. Garnish with chopped cilantro.

NUTRIENT PER PORTION	CALORIES	PROTEIN	CARBOHYDRATES	FAT	FIBRE	SODIUM
	399 kcal	31g	41g	12g	7g	116mg

Chicken Fried Rice

1 PORTION

PREP TIME: 5 minutes | **TOTAL TIME:** 20 minutes

INGREDIENTS:

- 1 large egg
- ¼ tsp black pepper
- 1 tsp (5 mL) canola oil
- 3 oz (85 g) raw boneless skinless chicken breast, chopped
- 1 medium carrot, shredded
- 1 garlic clove, minced
- 1 tsp ginger, grated
- 2 medium green onions, chopped
- 4 medium button mushrooms, halved and thinly sliced
- ½ medium red bell pepper, finely chopped
- ½ cup brown rice, cooked
- 1 tsp (5 mL) low sodium soy sauce

DIRECTIONS:

- Beat egg in a small bowl with black pepper.
- Heat oil in a medium skillet over medium high heat.
- Cook chicken for 4-5 minutes, stirring occasionally, until cooked through.
- Add the carrot, garlic, ginger, green onions, mushrooms, and red bell pepper.
- Cook for 1-2 minutes until vegetables just begin to soften.
- Add the rice and cook for 2-4 more minutes, stirring constantly, until the rice begins to crisp up. Push rice to edges of the pan, add beaten egg to the centre of the skillet and stir until egg is just set.
- Add the soy sauce and mix to combine.

NUTRIENT PER PORTION	CALORIES	PROTEIN	CARBOHYDRATES	FAT	FIBRE	SODIUM
	376 kcal	28g	39g	12g	6g	346mg

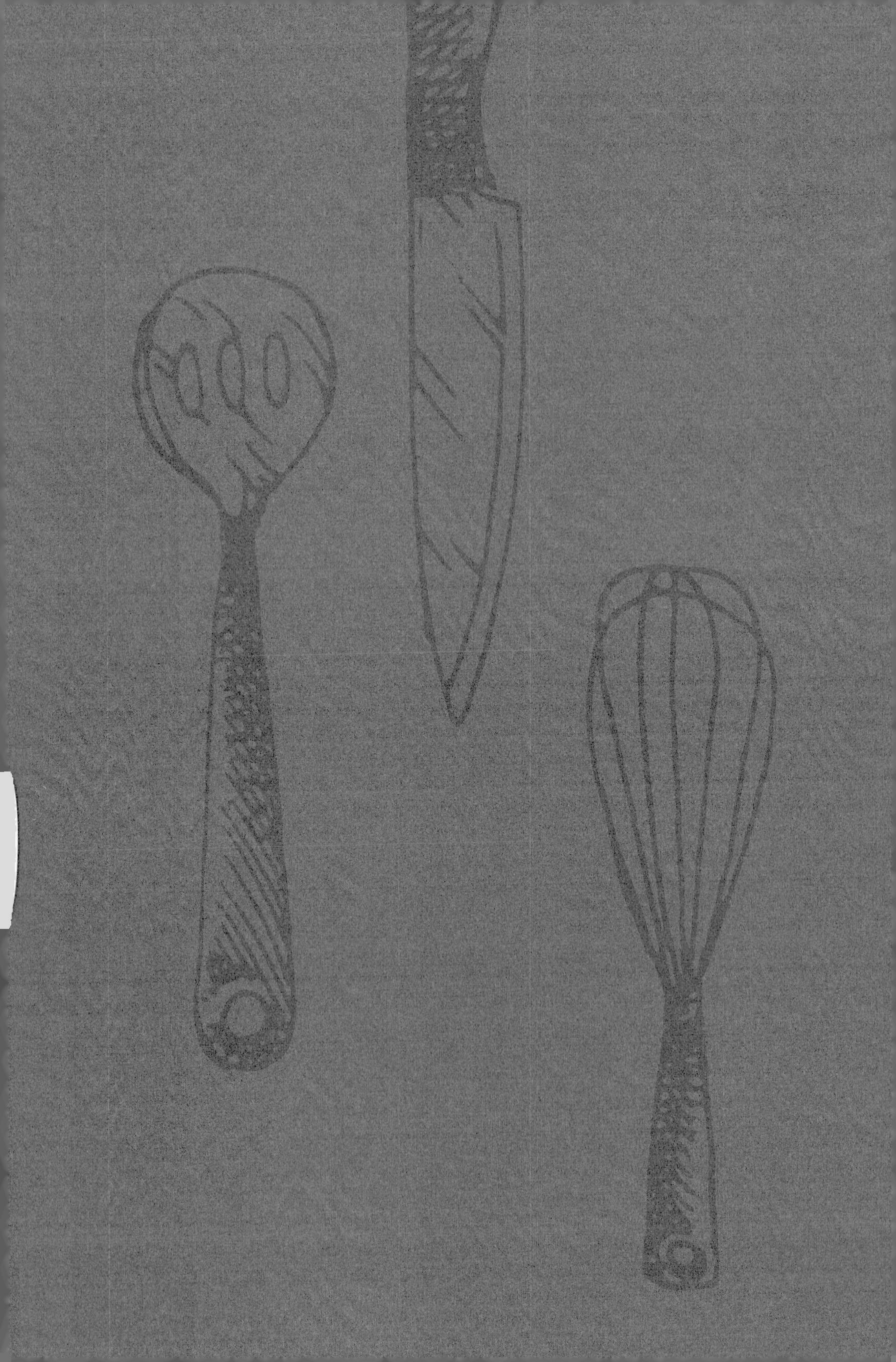

Dinner
RECIPES

Mac and Cheese Casserole

6 PORTIONS

PREP TIME: 30 minutes |

TOTAL TIME: 50 minutes

INGREDIENTS:

- 10 oz (283 g) dried whole wheat macaroni
- 1 lb (454 g) raw extra lean ground beef
- 2 tsp (10 mL) canola oil
- 1 large onion, chopped
- 2 medium red bell peppers, chopped
- 3 garlic cloves, minced
- ½ tsp black pepper
- 1 Tbsp. chili powder
- 1 tsp ground cumin
- 1 can (14 oz/398 mL) no sodium added crushed tomatoes
- ½ cup low fat cheddar cheese, shredded

DIRECTIONS:

- Preheat oven to 350°F (175°C).
- Cook the macaroni according to package directions; drain and set aside.
- Cook ground beef in a large skillet over medium heat until no longer pink; drain fat. Remove beef from skillet; set aside.
- Add oil to the same pan and heat over a medium heat.
- Cook onion and peppers for 3-4 minutes until translucent.
- Add garlic and cook for 1 minute more.
- Add the black pepper, chili powder, cumin, and crushed tomatoes.
- In a large bowl, combine the macaroni, beef, and tomato mixture.
- Spread the mixture into a greased 13 x 9-inch (3 L) baking dish.
- Top with the cheese and bake at 350°F for 20 to 25 minutes, or until the cheese is lightly browned and bubbly.

NUTRIENT PER PORTION	CALORIES	PROTEIN	CARBOHYDRATES	FAT	FIBRE	SODIUM
	370 kcal	29g	47g	9g	3g	200mg

Crowd-Pleasing Lasagna

10 PORTIONS

 **PREP TIME:** 1 hour |  **TOTAL TIME:** 2 hours

INGREDIENTS:

- 15 dried whole-wheat lasagna noodles
- 1 lb (454 g) raw extra lean ground beef
- 1 Tbsp. (15 mL) canola oil
- 8 medium button mushrooms, diced
- 2 medium carrots, shredded
- 1 small onion, chopped
- 1 medium zucchini, shredded
- 3 cloves of garlic, minced
- 2 cans (28 oz/796 mL) no sodium added tomato sauce
- 1 Tbsp. dried basil
- 1 large egg, lightly beaten
- 1 15 oz (425 g) container low fat ricotta cheese
- 1 10 oz (283 g) package frozen chopped spinach, thawed and squeezed of excess liquid
- ½ tsp freshly ground black pepper
- ⅛ tsp ground nutmeg
- ½ cup low fat mozzarella cheese, shredded

SIDE SALAD:

- 10 cups spring mix lettuce
- 2 cucumbers, chopped
- 3 medium tomatoes, chopped
- 3 Tbsp. (45 mL) olive oil
- 3 Tbsp. (45 mL) balsamic vinegar

DIRECTIONS:

- Preheat oven to 375°F (190°C).
- Place the slice of bread on the baking sheet.
- Cook ground beef in a large skillet over medium heat until no longer pink; drain fat. Remove beef from skillet; set aside.
- Add the oil to the same pan and heat over a medium-high heat. Add the mushrooms, carrot, onion, and zucchini and cook, stirring occasionally, until the vegetables are softened and browned, about 5-7 minutes. Add minced garlic and cook for another 1-2 minutes. Return the meat to the pan. Stir in 1 can of tomato sauce and basil; simmer for 10-15 minutes.
- While the meat sauce cooks, combine the egg, ricotta cheese, spinach, black pepper, and nutmeg in a medium-sized bowl; set aside.
- Spread ½ of the second can of tomato sauce on the bottom of a 13 x 9-inch (3 L) baking dish.
- Place a layer of lasagna noodles on top, touching but not overlapping.
- Spread one third of the ricotta mixture on top of the noodles, then spread one third of the meat sauce.
- Repeat noodles, ricotta and meat sauce for two more layers.
- Top the final layer of noodles with the remaining ½ can of tomato sauce and sprinkle on grated mozzarella.
- Cover loosely with foil and bake for 45 minutes. Remove foil and bake for 10 minutes more.
- Toss lettuce, cucumber, tomato, olive oil, and balsamic vinegar together to make a side salad and serve with lasagna.

NUTRIENT PER PORTION	CALORIES	PROTEIN	CARBOHYDRATES	FAT	FIBRE	SODIUM
	469 kcal	29g	54g	16g	12g	208mg

Hearty Chili

6 PORTIONS

PREP TIME: 30 minutes | 
TOTAL TIME: 1 hour

INGREDIENTS:

- 1 lb (454 g) raw extra lean ground beef
- 2 tsp (10 mL) canola oil
- 2 medium carrots, shredded
- 2 garlic cloves, minced
- 1 large onion, chopped
- 1 medium red bell pepper, chopped
- ½ tsp cayenne pepper
- 2 Tbsp. chili powder
- 2 tsp ground cumin
- 1 can (14 oz/398 mL) no sodium added kidney beans, drained and rinsed
- 1 can (14 oz/398 mL) no sodium added tomato sauce

SIDES:

- 6 cups spring mix lettuce
- 1 medium cucumber, chopped
- 2 medium tomatoes, chopped
- 2 Tbsp. (30 mL) olive oil
- 2 Tbsp. (30 mL) balsamic vinegar
- 6 small whole wheat dinner rolls

DIRECTIONS:

- Cook ground beef in a large skillet over medium heat until no longer pink; drain fat. Remove beef from skillet; set aside.
- Heat oil in a large soup pot or Dutch oven over medium heat.
- Add carrot, garlic, onion, and red bell pepper and cook, stirring frequently until softened, about 5 minutes.
- Add cayenne pepper, chili powder, and cumin; cook, stirring constantly, for 1 minute.
- Add cooked ground beef, kidney beans, tomato sauce, and 1 cup water; stir to combine.
- Bring to a boil, then lower heat to low. Cover and simmer, stirring often, until flavours have melded and sauce is thickened and bubbly, about 30 minutes.
- Toss lettuce, cucumber, tomato, olive oil and balsamic vinegar together to make a side salad.
- Ladle chili into bowls and serve with side salad and a whole wheat dinner roll.

NUTRIENT	CALORIES	PROTEIN	CARBOHYDRATES	FAT	FIBRE	SODIUM
PER PORTION	442 kcal	30g	51g	15g	12g	263mg

Weeknight Spaghetti Bolognese

6 PORTIONS

PREP TIME: 10 minutes | **TOTAL TIME:** 1 hour

INGREDIENTS:

- 1 lb (454 g) raw extra lean ground beef
- 1 tsp (5 mL) canola oil
- 1 small onion, diced
- 2 garlic cloves, minced
- 1 Tbsp. (15 mL) tomato paste
- 2 medium carrots, shredded
- 4 medium button mushrooms, diced
- 1 zucchini, cut into quarters lengthwise and thinly sliced
- ½ cup (125 mL) no sodium added beef broth
- 2 cans (28 oz/796 mL) no sodium added diced tomatoes
- 8 oz (227 g) dried whole wheat spaghetti

DIRECTIONS:

- Cook ground beef in a large skillet over medium heat until no longer pink; drain fat. Remove beef from skillet; set aside.
- Add oil to the same skillet and heat over medium heat.
- Cook onion for 3-4 minutes until translucent.
- Add garlic and cook for 1 minute more.
- Add tomato paste, carrots, mushrooms, zucchini and cook until the vegetables begin to soften, about 5-7 minutes.
- Add beef broth and diced tomatoes. Lower heat and simmer until thickened, approximately 20 minutes.
- Once the sauce has cooked for at least 20 minutes, cook the pasta al dente according to the directions on the package. Drain well and return pasta to the cooking pot.
- Add half of the sauce to the pasta and toss together.
- Transfer pasta to serving dishes and spoon remaining sauce over the pasta.

NUTRIENT	CALORIES	PROTEIN	CARBOHYDRATES	FAT	FIBRE	SODIUM
PER PORTION	320 kcal	25g	40g	8g	7g	90mg

Moussaka

6 PORTIONS

PREP TIME: 55 minutes | **TOTAL TIME:** 1 hour 35 minutes

INGREDIENTS:

- 1 lb (454 g) raw extra lean ground beef
- 2 tsp (10 mL) canola oil, divided
- 1 medium onion, chopped
- 2 garlic cloves, minced
- ½ tsp black pepper
- ¼ tsp cinnamon
- 2 tsp dried oregano
- 1 can (28 oz/796 mL) no sodium added diced tomatoes
- 1 eggplant, sliced into thin rounds
- 2 medium zucchini, sliced into thin rounds
- 2 large red skinned potatoes, washed and sliced into thin rounds
- 2 large eggs, lightly beaten
- ½ cup plain 2% Greek yogurt
- ½ cup low fat ricotta cheese
- ⅛ tsp ground nutmeg

DIRECTIONS:

- Preheat oven to 400°F (200°C).
- Cook ground beef in a large skillet over medium heat until no longer pink; drain fat. Remove beef from skillet; set aside.
- Add 1 tsp oil to the same pan and heat over medium heat.
- Cook onions for 3-4 minutes until translucent.
- Add garlic and cook for 1 minute more.
- Add cooked ground beef, black pepper, cinnamon, oregano, and diced tomatoes. Lower heat and simmer until thickened, approximately 20 minutes.
- Line two baking sheets with parchment paper.
- Lay the eggplant, zucchini, and potato in a single layer on the baking sheets and bake for 10 minutes or until just tender.
- Remove from oven and lower oven temperature to 350°F (175°C).
- Beat eggs in a bowl.
- Mix in Greek yogurt, ricotta cheese, and nutmeg.
- Grease a 13 x 9-inch (3 L) baking dish with remaining tsp of oil or line with parchment paper.
- Layer potato slices on the bottom of the pan, overlapping if necessary.
- Spread on half the meat sauce.
- Arrange eggplant and zucchini slices in an even layer on top of the meat sauce.
- Layer on remaining meat sauce.
- Top with cheese mixture.
- Bake, uncovered, for 40 minutes.
- Allow moussaka to cool for 5 minutes before slicing and serving.

NUTRIENT PER PORTION	CALORIES	PROTEIN	CARBOHYDRATES	FAT	FIBRE	SODIUM
	369 kcal	29g	38g	12g	9g	150mg

Steak Rice Bowl

1 PORTION

PREP TIME: 1 hour 10 minutes | **TOTAL TIME:** 1 hour 20 minutes

INGREDIENTS:

- 3 oz (85 g) raw eye of round steak
- 1 garlic clove, minced
- 1 tsp ginger, grated
- 2 medium button mushrooms, thinly sliced
- ¼ cup (60 mL) no sodium added beef broth
- 1 tsp (5 mL) unseasoned rice wine vinegar
- ¼ tsp red bell pepper flakes
- 2 tsp (10 mL) canola oil, divided
- 1 cup fresh spinach
- ½ cup brown rice, cooked
- 1 large egg
- 1 small carrot, grated
- ¼ small cucumber, thinly sliced into matchsticks
- 1 medium green onion, thinly sliced

DIRECTIONS:

- Add steak, garlic, ginger, mushrooms, beef broth, rice wine vinegar, and red bell pepper flakes to a food storage bag and seal.
- Mix ingredients in the bag and allow to marinate in the fridge for at least one hour or leave overnight.
- When ready to cook, heat 1 tsp oil in a medium skillet over a medium-high heat.
- Remove the steak from the marinade and cook for 3-4 minutes per side for medium rare or as desired; set aside to rest.
- Add the mushrooms and remaining marinade to the skillet; cook for 3-5 minutes or until softened.
- When mushrooms have cooked, add the spinach and stir until the spinach is wilted.
- Add the rice to a bowl and pour the mushrooms, spinach, and sauce over one section of the rice.
- In the same pan, heat the remaining tsp of oil over medium heat and fry the egg until the whites are set and the yolk is cooked to your liking.
- Slice steak very thinly against the grain.
- Place the steak, carrots, and cucumber on different sections of the rice.
- Top with egg and garnish with green onion.

NUTRIENT	CALORIES	PROTEIN	CARBOHYDRATES	FAT	FIBRE	SODIUM
PER PORTION	443 kcal	32g	36g	19g	5g	212mg

Homestyle Meatloaf

2 PORTIONS

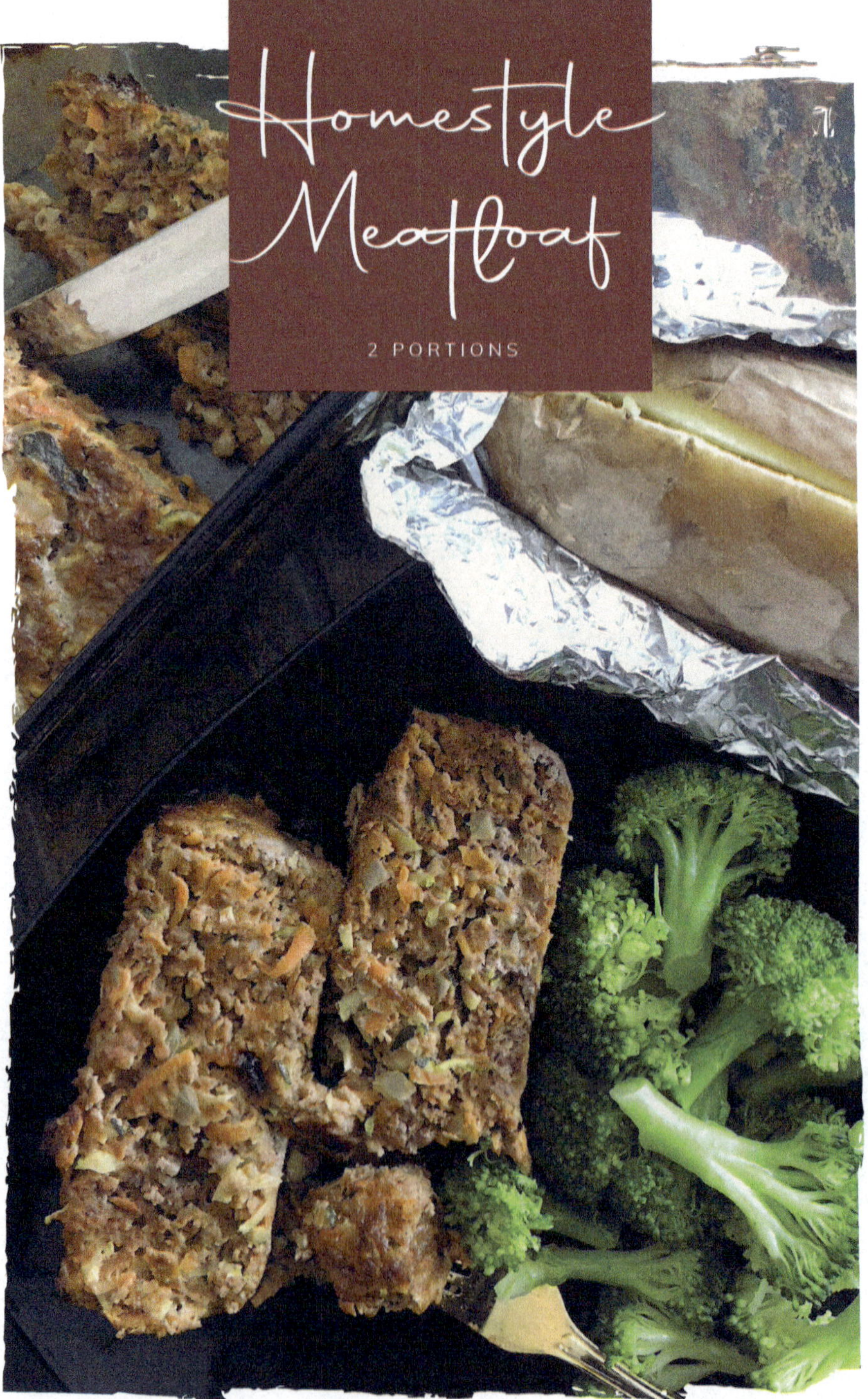

PREP TIME: 15 minutes | **TOTAL TIME:** 1 hour 45 minutes

INGREDIENTS:

- 2 tsp (10 mL) canola oil, divided
- 1 small onion, finely chopped
- 2 medium carrots, shredded
- 1 lb (454 g) raw extra lean ground beef
- 2 large eggs
- 1 medium zucchini, shredded
- ½ cup whole wheat breadcrumbs
- 1 tsp black pepper
- 2 Tbsp. (30 mL) Worcestershire sauce
- ½ cup (125 mL) no sodium added tomato sauce

SIDES:

- 1 medium sweet potato
- 2 cups broccoli florets, chopped

DIRECTIONS:

- Preheat oven to 400°F (200°C). Grease a 9 x 5-inch (1.9 L) loaf pan with 1 tsp oil.
- Heat remaining tsp of oil in a medium skillet over medium heat.
- Cook onions for 3-4 minutes until translucent.
- Add shredded carrots and cook until softened, approximately 3 minutes.
- Combine cooked carrots and onions, ground beef, eggs, zucchini, bread crumbs, black pepper, and Worcestershire in a large bowl; mix well using your hands. Press meat mixture into the prepared loaf pan.
- Bake for 75-90 minutes, or until cooked through.
- Wrap sweet potato in foil. Add the sweet potato to the oven and bake for 45 minutes.
- Steam broccoli until tender, 5-8 minutes.
- Spread tomato sauce on the top of the meatloaf once cooked and continue baking until bubbling, about 5 more minutes.
- Remove meatloaf and sweet potato from oven. Let meatloaf rest for 10 minutes before slicing into 8 slices.
- Slice sweet potato in half lengthwise.
- Divide sweet potato and broccoli between two plates and serve with meatloaf.

NUTRIENT	CALORIES	PROTEIN	CARBOHYDRATES	FAT	FIBRE	SODIUM
PER PORTION	418 kcal	34g	38g	15g	8g	346mg

Lamb Korma

4 PORTIONS

PREP TIME: 30 minutes |  **TOTAL TIME:** 4 hours 30 minutes

INGREDIENTS:

- ¾ cup brown Basmati rice, uncooked
- 1 Tbsp. (15 mL) canola oil
- 1 lb (454 g) raw boneless leg of lamb roast, trimmed of fat, chopped
- 2 bay leaves
- 1 cinnamon stick
- 1 tsp cardamom
- 1 Tbsp. ground coriander
- 1 Tbsp. ground cumin
- ⅛ tsp ground nutmeg
- 1 tsp turmeric
- 3 garlic cloves, minced
- 1 Tbsp. ginger, grated
- 2 medium onions, chopped
- 1 cup 2% plain Greek yogurt
- 4 medium carrots, chopped
- 4 celery stalks, chopped
- 2 medium tomatoes, chopped
- ½ cup fresh cilantro, chopped

DIRECTIONS:

- Cook rice according to package directions.
- Heat oil in a large skillet over medium heat.
- Brown lamb pieces for 2-3 minutes per side, transfer to a plate and set aside. Leave oil and lamb drippings in skillet.
- Add the bay leaves, cinnamon stick, cardamom, coriander, cumin, nutmeg, and turmeric to the skillet; cook for 2-3 minutes.
- Stir in garlic, ginger, and onions; cook until onions are soft, approximately 5 minutes.
- Transfer mixture to a slow cooker.
- Add browned lamb, Greek yogurt, carrots, celery, tomatoes and ½ cup water; stir to combine. Cover and cook on LOW for 4 hours or HIGH for 2 hours, or until the lamb is fork tender.
- Serve lamb korma over cooked rice and garnish with cilantro.

NUTRIENT PER PORTION	CALORIES	PROTEIN	CARBOHYDRATES	FAT	FIBRE	SODIUM
	421 kcal	27g	46g	16g	7g	145mg

Slow Cooker Pulled Pork Sandwiches

6 PORTIONS

PREP TIME: 30 minutes |  **TOTAL TIME:** 8 hours 30 minutes

INGREDIENTS:

- 2 lb (908 g) raw boneless lean pork shoulder roast
- 2 tsp (10 mL) canola oil
- 1 large onion, diced
- 4 garlic cloves, minced
- 1 tsp black pepper
- 2 Tbsp. chili powder
- ¼ cup (60 mL) cider vinegar
- ¼ cup (60 mL) tomato paste
- 1 Tbsp. (15 mL) Worcestershire sauce
- 1 cup (250 mL) no sodium added beef broth
- 6 whole wheat hamburger buns

COLESLAW:

- ½ cup plain 2% Greek yogurt
- 1 tsp ground cumin
- 2 Tbsp. (30 mL) lemon juice
- 6 cups savoy cabbage, shredded

DIRECTIONS:

- Use paper towels to pat the pork shoulder dry. Place the shoulder into a slow cooker.
- Heat oil in a large skillet over a medium-high heat.
- Add onion; cook for about 4 minutes or until soft.
- Add the garlic, cook for a minute more.
- Stir in the black pepper, chili powder, cider vinegar, tomato paste, and Worcestershire sauce.
- Cook until most of the vinegar has evaporated and the mixture has thickened, about 5-10 minutes.
- Rub the onion mixture all over the pork shoulder, then pour the beef broth into the slow cooker.
- Cover and cook on LOW for 8 hours or HIGH for 4 hours, or until the meat is very tender.
- Use two forks to pull the meat apart, then stir it into the cooking juices.
- Mix together Greek yogurt, cumin and lemon juice; pour over cabbage and mix.
- Spoon pulled pork onto hamburger buns and top with coleslaw.

NUTRIENT PER PORTION	CALORIES	PROTEIN	CARBOHYDRATES	FAT	FIBRE	SODIUM
	422 kcal	38g	35g	15g	7g	434mg

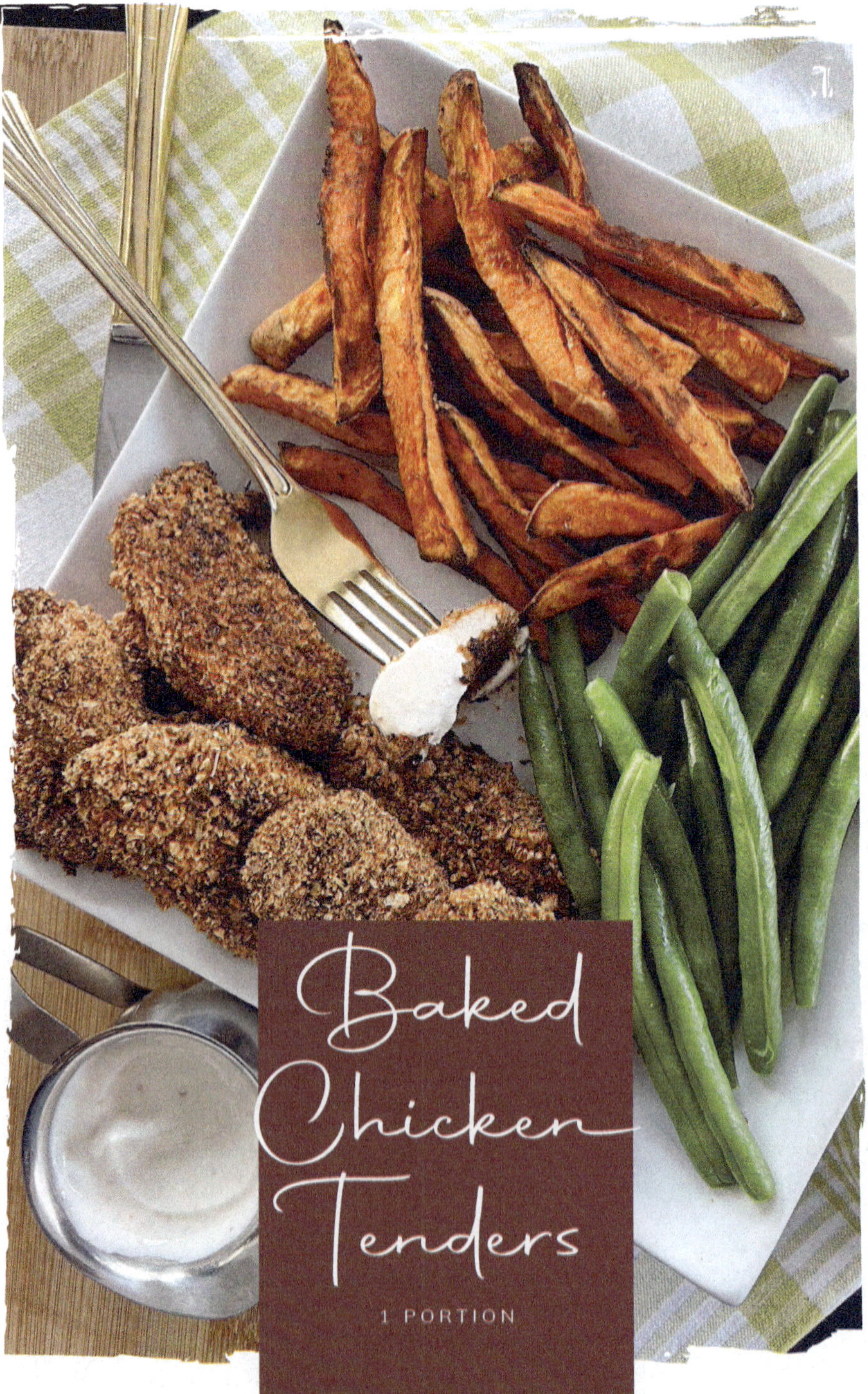

Baked Chicken Tenders

1 PORTION

PREP TIME: 15 minutes | **TOTAL TIME:** 1 hour

INGREDIENTS:

- 1 tsp (5 mL) canola oil
- ½ tsp garlic powder
- ½ tsp paprika
- ¼ cup whole wheat bread crumbs
- ¼ tsp black pepper
- 1 tsp dried thyme
- 1 tsp (5 mL) Dijon mustard
- 4 oz (113 g) raw chicken tenders or breast, sliced
- 1 cup green beans, trimmed

FRIES:

- 1 medium sweet potato
- 1 tsp (5 mL) canola oil
- ½ tsp garlic powder
- ½ tsp paprika

DIPPING SAUCE:

- ¼ cup plain 2% Greek yogurt
- ¼ tsp ground cumin
- 1 Tbsp. (15 mL) lemon juice

DIRECTIONS:

- Preheat oven to 400°F (200°C). Line a baking sheet with foil and grease with 1 tsp oil.
- Scrub sweet potato and cut into narrow fries, leaving skin on. Toss fries in a bowl with 1 tsp oil. Sprinkle with 1/2 tsp each garlic powder and paprika.
- Spread fries out on half of the baking sheet and roast for 20 minutes.
- In a small bowl mix together 1/2 tsp garlic powder, 1/2 tsp paprika, bread crumbs, black pepper, and thyme.
- Spread Dijon mustard over the chicken tenders so they are lightly coated. Dip the chicken in the seasoned bread crumbs and roll around until evenly coated.
- After the fries have baked for 20 minutes, flip them and add the chicken tenders to the other half of the baking sheet. Cook 20 minutes more, flipping chicken halfway through, or until chicken is cooked through and fries are slightly crispy.
- Steam green beans for 8-10 minutes or until tender.
- Mix together dipping sauce ingredients in a small bowl.
- Serve chicken fingers with sweet potato fries, green beans and dipping sauce.

NUTRIENT PER PORTION	CALORIES	PROTEIN	CARBOHYDRATES	FAT	FIBRE	SODIUM
	442 kcal	39g	42g	14g	9g	399 mg

Chicken and Mushroom Stew

6 PORTIONS

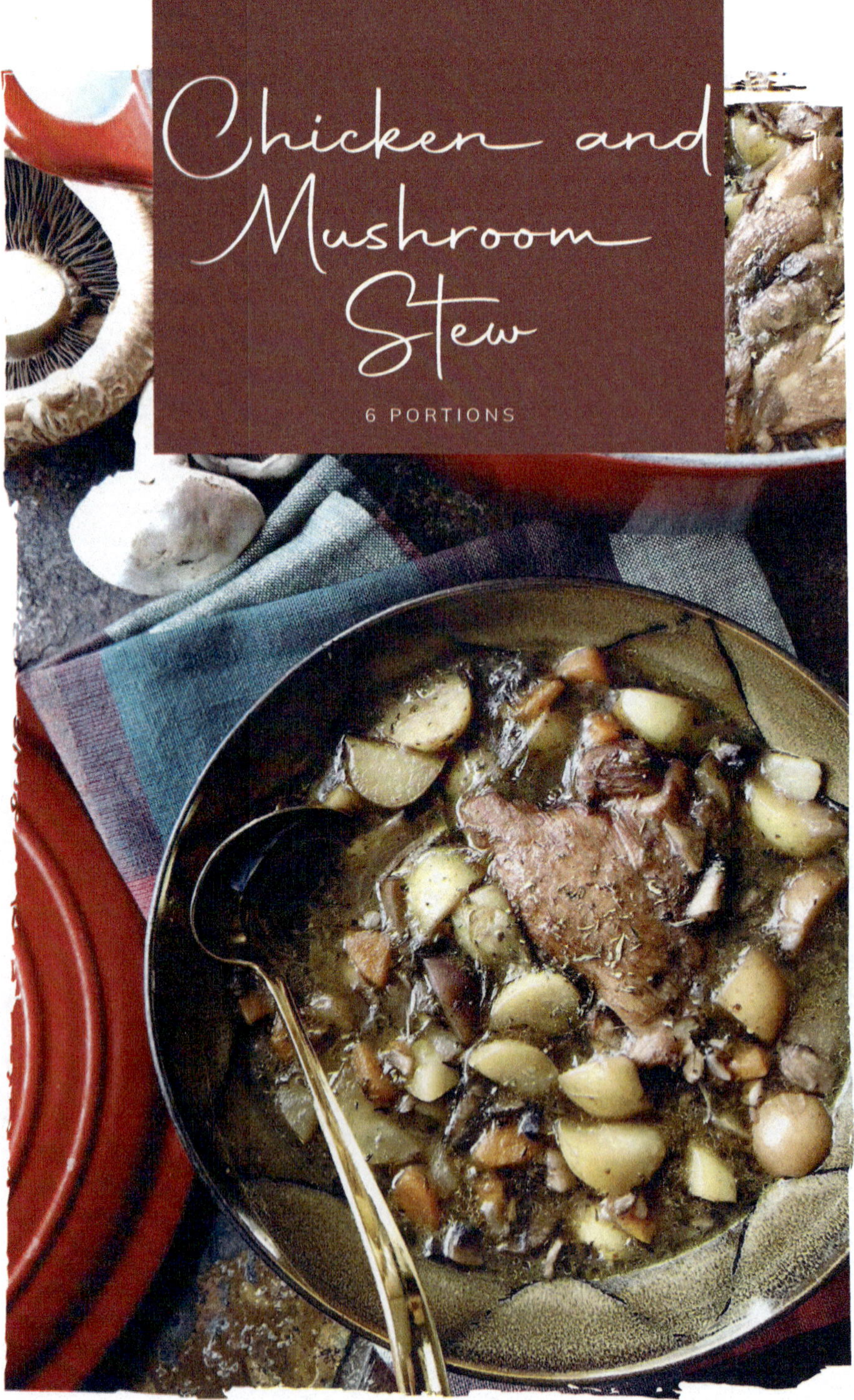

PREP TIME: 20 minutes | **TOTAL TIME:** 1 hour 20 minutes

INGREDIENTS:

- 2 Tbsp. (30 mL) canola oil, divided
- 8 raw skinless bone-in chicken thighs
- 2 large onions, chopped
- 1 lb (454 g) medium button mushrooms, quartered
- 2 Portobello mushrooms, chopped
- 2 medium carrots, chopped
- 2 lb creamer potatoes, chopped
- 1 tsp black pepper
- 1 Tbsp. dried thyme
- 2 cup (500 mL) no sodium added chicken broth
- 1 cup (250 mL) dry red wine*

DIRECTIONS:

- Heat 1 Tbsp. oil in a large skillet over a medium-high heat.
- Brown chicken thighs in batches for 2-3 minutes per side and set aside. Pour out fat into a disposable container.
- Add remaining Tbsp. oil to the same pan and heat over medium heat.
- Cook the onions, button mushrooms, and Portobello mushrooms for 5 minutes or until they begin to brown.
- Add browned chicken, carrots, potatoes, black pepper, thyme, chicken broth, and red wine.
- Bring to a gentle simmer, cover the pan and simmer slowly until the meat and vegetables are very tender, at least one hour.

*Note: May substitute red wine with no sodium added chicken broth, if desired.

NUTRIENT	CALORIES	PROTEIN	CARBOHYDRATES	FAT	FIBRE	SODIUM
PER PORTION	426 kcal	34g	37g	13g	7g	137mg

Chicken Sweet Potato Enchiladas

CONTRIBUTED BY:
KATHERINE FORD, MSC, RD
8 PORTIONS

 **PREP TIME:** 20 minutes |  **TOTAL TIME:** 1 hour 20 minutes

NUTRIENT	CALORIES	PROTEIN	CARBOHYDRATES	FAT	FIBRE	SODIUM
PER PORTION	364 kcal	27g	50g	7g	12g	147mg

INGREDIENTS:

- 1 large sweet potato, peeled and diced
- 2 Tbsp. olive oil, divided
- 3 garlic cloves, minced
- 1 lb (454 g) raw boneless skinless chicken breast
- 1 small onion, chopped
- 1 can (14 oz/398 mL) each of no sodium added black beans and pinto beans, drained and rinsed
- 1 can (14 oz/398 mL) no sodium added tomato sauce
- 2 tsp dried oregano, divided
- 10 5-inch (13 cm) soft corn tortillas
- 1 cup low fat cheddar cheese, shredded
- ½ cup green onion, chopped

SIDES:

- 1.5 lb (680 g) fresh green beans, trimmed
- 1 cup plain 2% Greek yogurt

DIRECTIONS:

- Preheat oven to 375°F (190°C). Line one baking sheet with foil and one with parchment paper.
- Toss diced sweet potato in 1 Tbsp. oil and garlic. Spread on foil-lined baking sheet. Place chicken breast on parchment-lined baking sheet.
- Bake sweet potato and chicken for 25-30 minutes or until sweet potatoes are tender and chicken is cooked through.
- Transfer sweet potatoes into a large bowl and mash; set aside.
- Shred chicken using two forks; set aside.
- Heat the remaining Tbsp. of oil in a skillet over medium heat.
- Add the onion and cook for 4 minutes or until softened.
- Add the chicken, onion, and beans to the mashed sweet potato; stir to combine.
- Spread ½ the can of tomato sauce on the bottom of a 13 x 9-inch (3 L) baking dish. Sprinkle with 1 tsp of oregano.
- Warm the tortillas in the microwave for about 20 seconds to help prevent them from cracking.
- Fill the centre of each tortilla with a few spoonfuls of filling. Roll the tortilla and place seam-down in the baking dish.
- Cover the enchiladas with the remaining tomato sauce and any remaining filling.
- Sprinkle remaining oregano over the sauce. Top with shredded cheese and green onions.
- Cover with foil and bake for 20 minutes. Uncover and bake for 5 minutes more.
- Steam green beans for 8-10 minutes or until tender.
- Top enchiladas with Greek yogurt and serve with green beans.

One Pan Chicken Fajitas

2 PORTIONS

PREP TIME: 10 minutes | **TOTAL TIME:** 30 minutes

INGREDIENTS:

- 1 ½ tsp (7.5 mL) canola oil, divided
- 1 tsp chili powder
- 1 tsp ground cumin
- ½ tsp onion powder
- 4 oz (113 g) raw boneless skinless chicken breast, sliced into thin strips
- 1 small onion, thinly sliced
- 2 small red bell peppers, thinly sliced
- 2 5-inch (13 cm) soft corn or whole wheat tortillas
- 2 Tbsp. fresh cilantro, chopped
- 1 Tbsp. (15 mL) lime juice
- 2 Tbsp. plain 2% Greek yogurt

DIRECTIONS:

- Preheat oven to 425°F (220°C). Line a baking sheet with foil and grease with ½ tsp oil.
- Mix chili powder, cumin and onion powder in a small bowl.
- In a large bowl, mix chicken, onion, and peppers with remaining 1 tsp oil. Add seasoning mix and toss to coat.
- Spread in a single layer on the baking sheet and bake until chicken is cooked and vegetables are tender crisp, about 10-15 minutes.
- Wrap tortillas in foil and warm in oven for the last 5 minutes of cooking.
- Remove fajita filling from oven and transfer to a serving dish.
- Divide fajita filing equally onto each corn tortilla.
- Sprinkle with cilantro and lime juice. Top each fajita with Greek yogurt.

*Note: Nutrient analysis done with corn tortillas.

NUTRIENT PER PORTION	CALORIES	PROTEIN	CARBOHYDRATES	FAT	FIBRE	SODIUM
	343 kcal	33g	34g	9g	6g	124mg

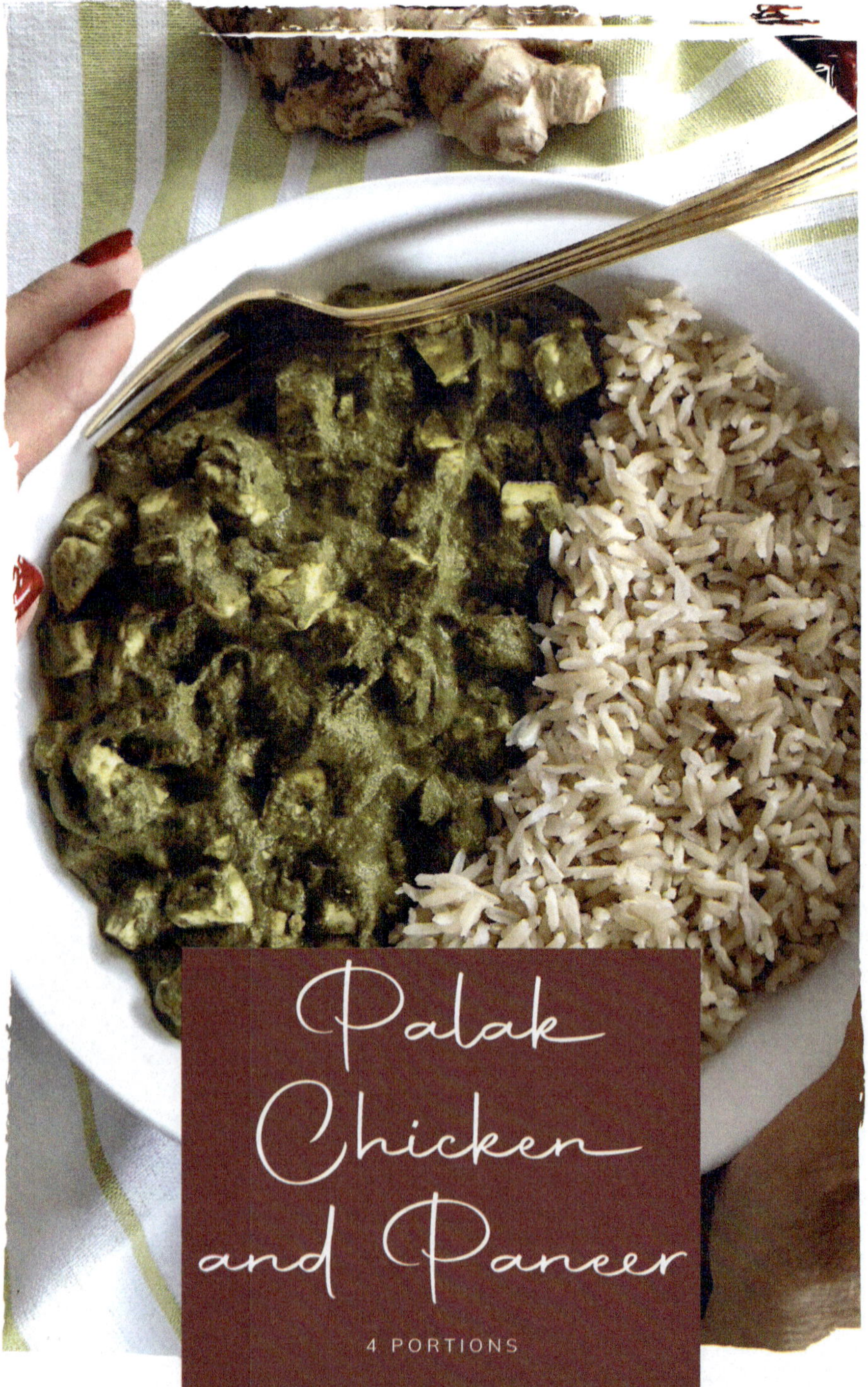

Palak Chicken and Paneer

4 PORTIONS

PREP TIME: 10 minutes | **TOTAL TIME:** 40 minutes

INGREDIENTS:

- ¾ cup brown rice, uncooked
- 2 tsp (10 mL) canola oil
- 6 oz (170 g) raw boneless, skinless chicken breast, cubed
- 3 garlic cloves, minced
- 2 tsp ginger, grated
- 2 tsp garam masala
- 1 tsp ground coriander
- 1 tsp ground cumin
- 1 large onion, minced
- 1 Serrano chili pepper, minced
- 3 medium tomatoes, diced
- 1 lb (454 g) frozen chopped spinach, thawed and squeezed of excess liquid
- 1 cup plain 2% Greek yogurt
- 6 oz (170 g) cubed paneer

DIRECTIONS:

- Cook rice according to package directions; set aside.
- Heat oil in a large skillet over a medium heat. Cook chicken for 4-5 minutes or until cooked through. Transfer to a plate and set aside.
- In the remaining oil in the skillet, sauté the garlic, ginger, garam masala, coriander, and cumin for 1 minute.
- Add the onion and chili pepper and cook until soft, approximately 5 minutes.
- Stir in tomatoes and cook for 10 minutes. Add the spinach to the skillet and cook for 3-5 minutes.
- Transfer the mixture to a blender or food processor and add Greek yogurt. Blend until smooth.
- Return mixture to skillet. Add the paneer and cooked chicken; cover and simmer for 10 minutes.
- Serve with cooked rice.

NUTRIENT PER PORTION	CALORIES	PROTEIN	CARBOHYDRATES	FAT	FIBRE	SODIUM
	452 kcal	33g	44g	17g	7g	145mg

Greek Turkey Burgers

4 PORTIONS

PREP TIME: 15 minutes | **TOTAL TIME:** 30 minutes

INGREDIENTS:

- 1 lb (454 g) raw lean ground turkey
- 1 large egg
- 5 oz (142 g) frozen chopped spinach, squeezed of excess liquid
- 2 garlic cloves, minced
- ⅓ cup feta cheese, crumbled
- 2 tsp (10 mL) canola oil
- ½ medium red onion, thinly sliced
- 2 medium tomatoes, sliced
- 4 whole wheat hamburger buns

YOGURT SPREAD:

- ½ cup plain 2% Greek yogurt
- ¼ cup cucumber, finely chopped
- 1 tsp dried dill
- 1 Tbsp. (15 mL) lemon juice

SIDES:

- 2 medium red bell peppers, cut into quarters lengthwise
- 2 medium zucchini, cut in half widthwise then sliced into strips

DIRECTIONS:

- In a large bowl combine ground turkey, egg, spinach, garlic, and feta cheese.
- Divide the mixture into 4 portions and form each into a patty.
- Heat grill or barbeque to medium. Cook patties for 12-15 minutes, flipping halfway, or until cooked through.
- Cook red bell peppers and zucchini on grill or barbeque to desired tenderness.
- Combine yogurt spread ingredients in a small bowl.
- Spread bottom hamburger buns with yogurt spread.
- Top with red onion, tomato, and a burger patty. Serve with grilled vegetables.

NUTRIENT PER PORTION	CALORIES	PROTEIN	CARBOHYDRATES	FAT	FIBRE	SODIUM
	441 kcal	35g	37g	19g	7g	508mg

Shakshuka

4 PORTIONS

PREP TIME: 30 minutes | **TOTAL TIME:** 40 minutes

INGREDIENTS:

- 1 Tbsp. (15 mL) canola oil
- 8 oz (227 g) raw boneless skinless chicken breast, chopped
- 1 small onion, chopped
- 1 medium red bell pepper, chopped
- 4 garlic cloves, minced
- 3 Tbsp. (45 mL) tomato paste
- 2 tsp ground cumin
- 1 tsp ground coriander
- 1 tsp paprika
- ¼ tsp cinnamon
- ¼ tsp red pepper flakes
- ¼ tsp black pepper
- 1 can (14 oz/398 mL) no sodium added diced tomatoes
- 4 large eggs
- ¼ cup feta cheese, crumbled
- 2 Tbsp. fresh parsley, chopped

SIDE:

- 4 slices whole wheat bread, toasted

DIRECTIONS:

- Preheat oven to 400°F (200°C).
- Heat oil in a large ovenproof high-sided skillet over medium heat.
- Cook chicken for 4-5 minutes, stirring occasionally, until cooked through.
- Add onion, red bell pepper, garlic, tomato paste, cumin, coriander, paprika, cinnamon, red pepper flakes, and black pepper.
- Cook, stirring occasionally, for 3-5 minutes or until vegetables start to soften.
- Add diced tomatoes to skillet; cook, stirring occasionally, for 10 minutes or until thickened.
- Reduce heat to medium-low. Using a spoon, make 4 wells in the sauce mixture. Crack an egg into each well.
- Transfer skillet to oven; bake until eggs are cooked to desired doneness, approximately 8-10 minutes.
- Garnish with cheese and parsley. Serve with toast.

NUTRIENT PER PORTION	CALORIES	PROTEIN	CARBOHYDRATES	FAT	FIBRE	SODIUM
	326 kcal	25g	27g	13g	6g	371mg

Thai Coconut Fish Curry

4 PORTIONS

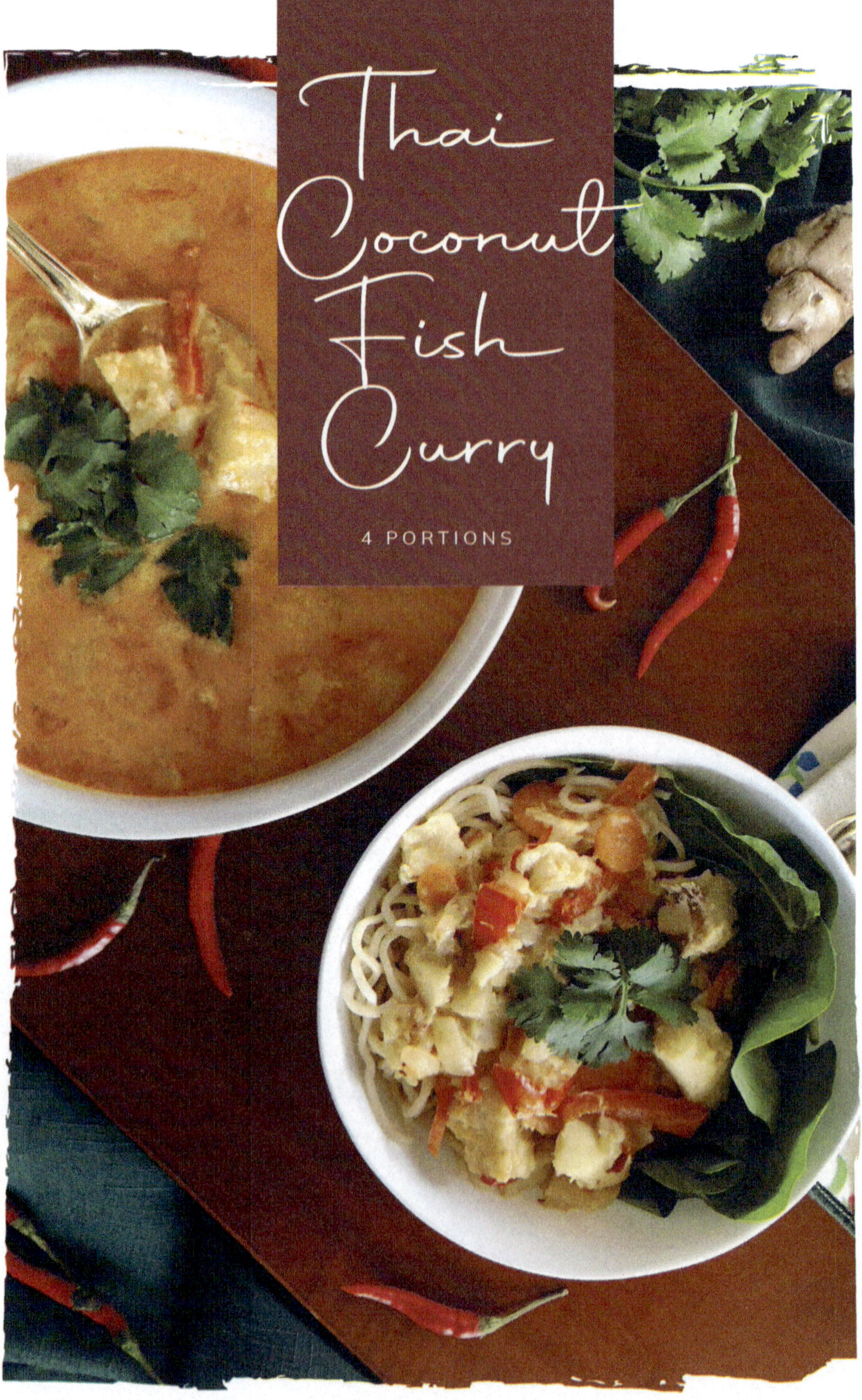

PREP TIME: 10 minutes | **TOTAL TIME:** 40 minutes

INGREDIENTS:

- 1 Tbsp. (15 mL) canola oil
- 1 large onion, chopped
- 2 Tbsp. ginger, grated
- 3 garlic cloves, minced
- 2 medium carrots, cut into thin coins
- 2 medium red bell peppers, thinly sliced
- 1 fresh Thai red chili, finely chopped
- ¼ cup (60 mL) no sodium added chicken broth
- 2 Tbsp. (30 mL) Thai red curry paste
- 1 can (14 oz/398 mL) light coconut milk
- 4 6-oz (170 g) fresh or frozen and thawed cod fillets, cubed
- 4 oz (113 g) dried rice noodles
- 4 cups fresh spinach
- 1 Tbsp. (15 mL) lime juice
- 1 cup fresh cilantro, chopped

DIRECTIONS:

- Heat oil in a large skillet with deep sides over medium heat.
- Add the onion and cook for 5 minutes or until softened.
- Add the ginger and garlic and cook for 1 minute more, stirring continuously.
- Add the carrots, red bell pepper, Thai red chili, and chicken broth.
- Cook, stirring occasionally, until the vegetables are just tender, approximately 8-10 minutes.
- Add the curry paste and cook, stirring often, until fragrant, about 2-3 minutes.
- Add the coconut milk and stir to combine.
- Bring the mixture to a simmer over medium heat.
- Add the fish and cook for 8-10 minutes, or until the fish flakes easily with a fork.
- Cook noodles according to package directions.
- Drain well and divide the noodles evenly between 4 bowls. Divide the spinach between the bowls.
- Remove the large skillet from the heat and stir in lime juice.
- Ladle the soup into the bowls and garnish with cilantro.

NUTRIENT PER PORTION	CALORIES	PROTEIN	CARBOHYDRATES	FAT	FIBRE	SODIUM
	409 kcal	30g	44g	12g	4g	801mg

Shrimp and Asparagus Risotto

4 PORTIONS

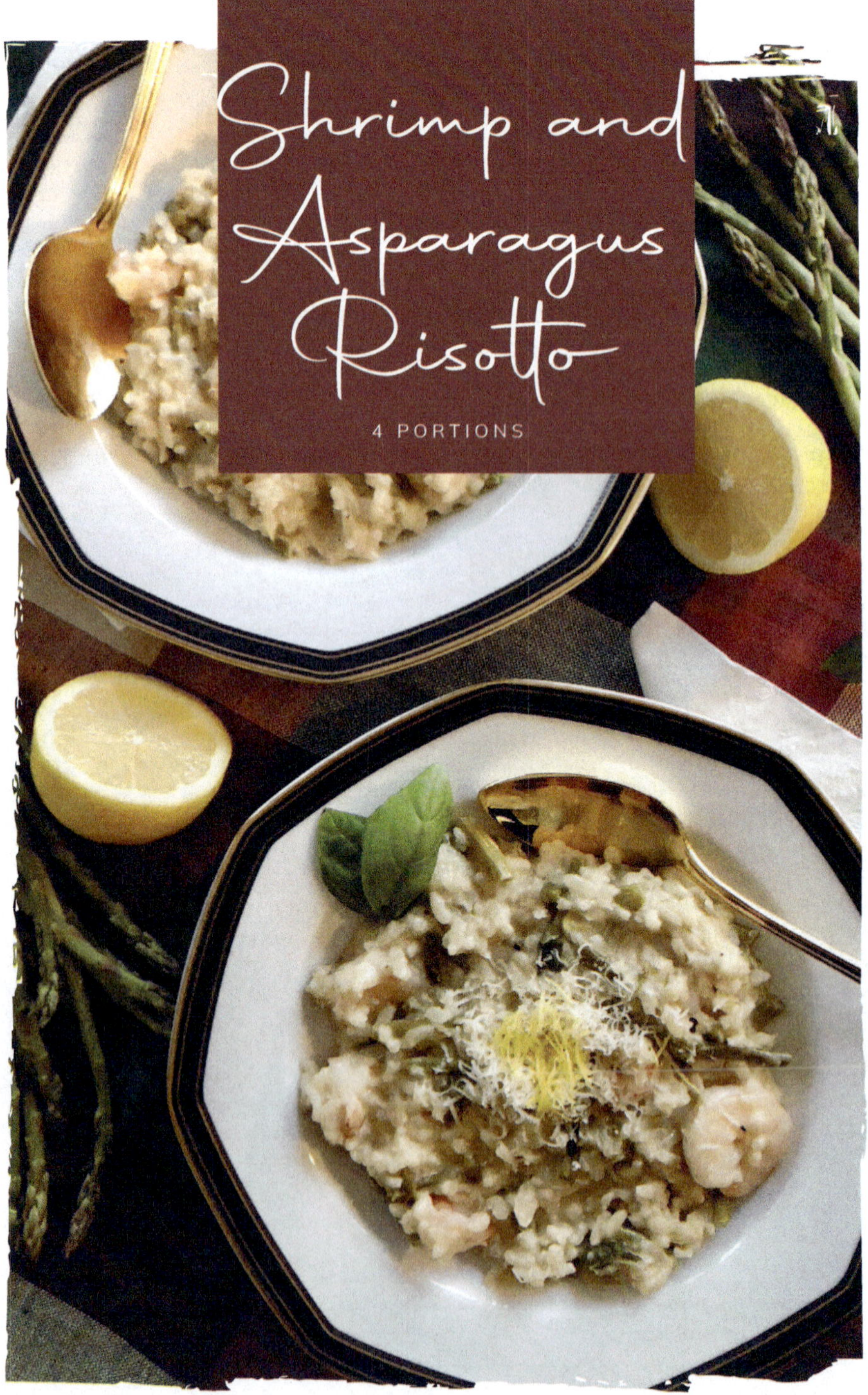

PREP TIME: 10 minutes | **TOTAL TIME:** 50 minutes

INGREDIENTS:

- 4 cups (1 L) no sodium added chicken broth
- 1 lb peeled and deveined shrimp, frozen and thawed or fresh
- 1 Tbsp. unsalted butter
- 1 Tbsp. (15 mL) canola oil
- 1 small onion, finely chopped
- 2 garlic cloves, minced
- 1 cup Arborio rice, uncooked
- ½ cup (125 mL) dry white wine
- 1 lb (454 g) asparagus, woody ends trimmed and cut into 1-inch (2.5 cm) pieces
- ¼ cup goat cheese
- 2 Tbsp. fresh Parmesan cheese, grated
- ¼ cup fresh basil, chopped
- ½ tsp black pepper
- 1 lemon, zest and juice

DIRECTIONS:

- Bring the broth to a simmer in a medium pot.
- Add the shrimp; cover and simmer over medium heat until just cooked, about 2 minutes. Transfer the shrimp to a plate to cool.
- Cover the broth and keep it at a gentle simmer.
- Heat butter and oil in a medium skillet over medium heat.
- Add the onion and cook approximately 4 minutes or until softened.
- Add the garlic and cook for 1 minute more.
- Stir in rice and cook for a couple minutes to toast the rice.
- Pour in the wine and simmer until almost evaporated, approximately 3 minutes.
- Add the asparagus and 1 cup of the broth and cook, stirring constantly, until it is absorbed.
- Continue to add the broth, 1 cup at a time, stirring constantly until it is absorbed. The risotto is done when the rice is tender but still slightly firm and creamy, approximately 25 minutes total.
- Once the rice is cooked, stir in the goat cheese and shrimp.
- Remove the risotto from the heat and stir in the Parmesan, basil, black pepper, lemon zest and lemon juice.

NUTRIENT	CALORIES	PROTEIN	CARBOHYDRATES	FAT	FIBRE	SODIUM
PER PORTION	450 kcal	33g	43g	12g	5g	259mg

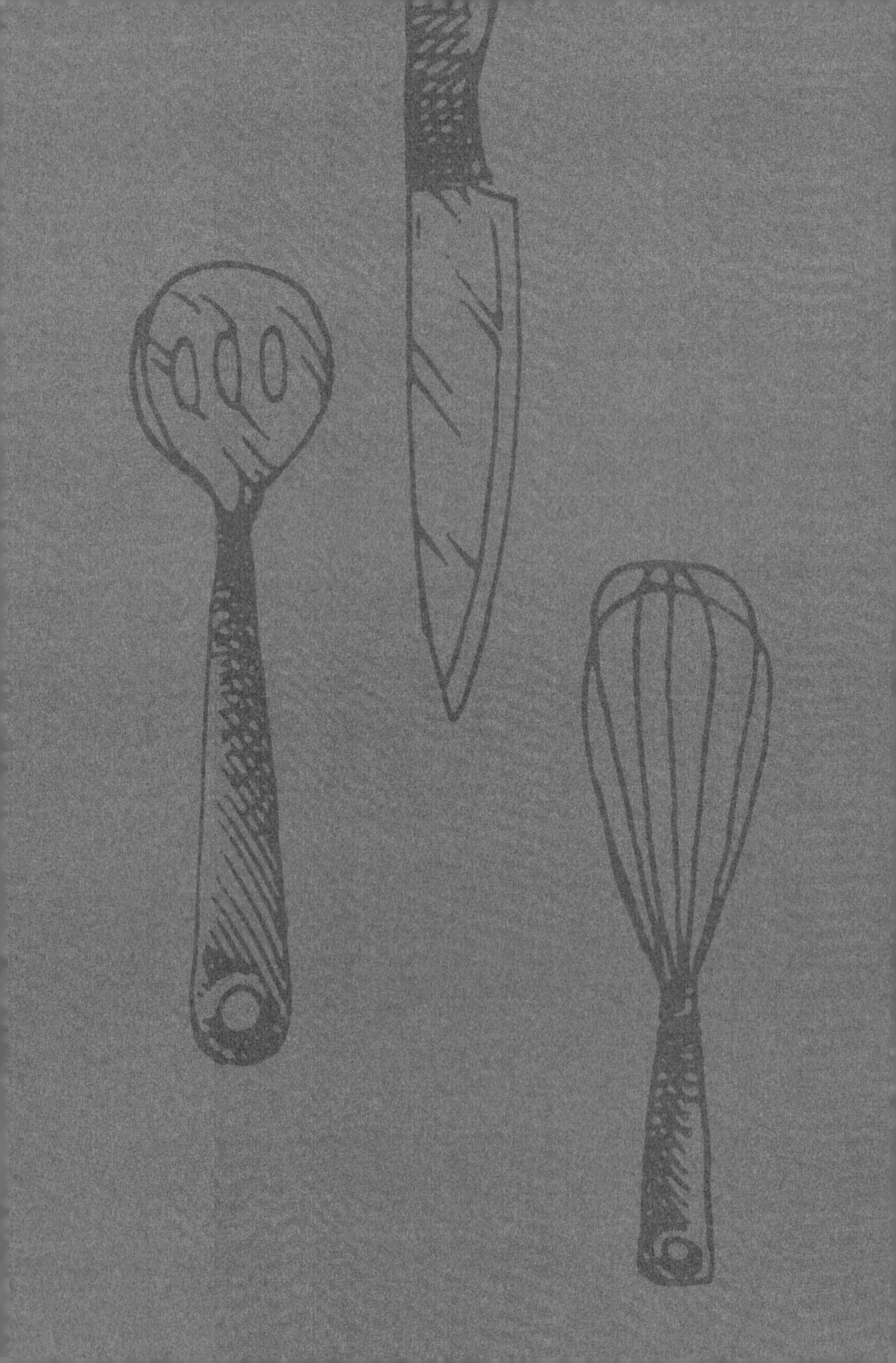

Snacks RECIPES

Tuna Melts

1 PORTION

 **PREP TIME:** 5 minutes |  **TOTAL TIME:** 15 minutes

INGREDIENTS:

- 1 slice whole wheat bread or bun*
- ¼ can (30 g) low sodium tuna, drained
- 1 Tbsp. plain 2% Greek yogurt
- ⅛ tsp black pepper
- ½ tsp dried dill
- 2 Tbsp. green onion, diced
- 2 Tbsp. red bell pepper, diced
- 2 Tbsp. partly skimmed mozzarella cheese, shredded

DIRECTIONS:

- Preheat oven to 400°F (200°C). Line a baking sheet with foil.
- Place the slice of bread on the baking sheet.
- Mix together the tuna, Greek yogurt, black pepper, and dill in a bowl.
- Lightly fold in the green onion and red bell pepper.
- Spoon over the slice of bread and top with shredded cheese.
- Bake until the cheese is melted and bread is toasted, about 8-10 minutes.

*Note: Nutrient analysis done with whole wheat bread.

NUTRIENT	CALORIES	PROTEIN	CARBOHYDRATES	FAT	FIBRE	SODIUM
PER PORTION	186 kcal	20g	16g	4g	3g	276mg

Mini Pizzas

1 PORTION

 **PREP TIME:** 5 minutes |  **TOTAL TIME:** 15 minutes

INGREDIENTS:

- 1 oz (28 g) cooked extra lean ground beef
- 1 thin style whole wheat bun
- 2 Tbsp. (30 mL) no sodium added canned tomato sauce
- ¼ tsp dried oregano
- 2 Tbsp. low fat mozzarella cheese, shredded
- 2 Tbsp. red bell pepper, diced

DIRECTIONS:

- Preheat oven to 400°F (200°C). Line a baking sheet with foil.
- Slice through the bun and place each cut side up on the foil.
- Spread 1 Tbsp. of tomato sauce on each half of the bun and sprinkle with oregano.
- Top each half with 1 Tbsp. each of ground beef, cheese, and red bell pepper.
- Bake until the cheese is melted and bun is toasted, about 8-10 minutes.

NUTRIENT	CALORIES	PROTEIN	CARBOHYDRATES	FAT	FIBRE	SODIUM
PER PORTION	195 kcal	13g	24g	6g	5g	260mg

Mini Frittatas

6 PORTIONS

 **PREP TIME:** 10 minutes |  **TOTAL TIME:** 40 minutes

INGREDIENTS:

- 2 tsp (10 mL) canola oil
- ½ cup russet potato, peeled and diced into ¼ inch cubes
- 8 large eggs
- ½ cup (125 mL) 2% milk
- ¼ tsp black pepper
- ½ cup low fat cheddar cheese, shredded
- ½ cup fresh or frozen spinach, squeezed of excess liquid

DIRECTIONS:

- Preheat oven to 375°F (195°C). Coat the inside of 6 muffin tins with oil.
- Boil the diced potatoes for 10 minutes or until fork tender; drain and set aside.
- Whisk the eggs, milk, and black pepper together in a large bowl.
- Sprinkle cheese, spinach and potatoes into each muffin tin.
- Pour egg mixture evenly into the muffin tins (about ¾ full) and bake for 15-20 minutes, or until lightly brown on top and fully set.

NUTRIENT	CALORIES	PROTEIN	CARBOHYDRATES	FAT	FIBRE	SODIUM
PER PORTION	157 kcal	12g	5g	10g	1g	171mg

Chili Cheese Potato Wedges

6 PORTIONS

 **PREP TIME:** 10 minutes |  **TOTAL TIME:** 1 hour

INGREDIENTS:

- 1 lb (454 g) raw extra lean ground beef
- 1 Tbsp. (15 mL) canola oil
- 2 medium carrots, shredded
- 2 celery stalks, finely chopped
- 2 cloves garlic, minced
- 1 large onion, chopped
- ½ tsp cayenne pepper
- 2 Tbsp. chili powder
- 2 tsp ground cumin
- 1 can (14 oz/398 mL) no sodium added tomato sauce
- 1 cup low fat cheddar cheese, shredded
- 4 medium green onions, thinly sliced
- 2 medium tomatoes, finely chopped
- ½ cup plain 2% Greek yogurt

FRIES:

- 3 small russet potatoes, cut into wedges
- 1 Tbsp. (15 mL) canola oil
- ½ tsp black pepper
- 1 Tbsp. dried thyme
- 1 tsp garlic powder
- 1 tsp onion powder

DIRECTIONS:

- Preheat oven to 400°F (200°C). Line a baking sheet with foil.
- Toss potato wedges with 1 Tbsp. oil, black pepper, thyme, garlic powder, and onion powder.
- Spread potato wedges on baking sheet and bake for 40 minutes, flipping halfway, or until tender and browned.
- Cook ground beef in a large skillet over medium heat until no longer pink; drain fat. Remove beef from skillet; set aside.
- Heat 1 Tbsp. oil in a large soup pot or Dutch oven over medium heat.
- Add carrot, celery, garlic, and onion.
- Cook, stirring frequently, for 5 minutes or until softened.
- Add cayenne pepper, chili powder, cumin. Cook, stirring constantly, for 1 minute.
- Add ground beef, tomato sauce, and 1 cup water; stir to combine.
- Bring to a boil then reduce heat to low. Cover and simmer, stirring often, for 30 minutes or until flavours have melded and sauce is thickened and bubbly.
- Divide potato wedges between 4 bowls. Ladle chili over potato wedges.
- Top each bowl with ¼ cup shredded cheese and microwave for 30 seconds on HIGH or until cheese is melted.
- Garnish with green onion, tomato, and Greek yogurt.

NUTRIENT	CALORIES	PROTEIN	CARBOHYDRATES	FAT	FIBRE	SODIUM
PER PORTION	356 kcal	28g	33g	13g	6g	241mg

Roast Beef and Cheese Wrap

2 PORTIONS

 **PREP TIME:** 5 minutes |  **TOTAL TIME:** 5 minutes

INGREDIENTS:

- 1 tsp (5mL) yellow mustard
- 1 8-inch (20 cm) whole wheat flour tortilla
- 2 oz (57 g) lean low sodium roast beef, sliced
- 1 oz (28 g) low fat brick cheddar cheese, sliced
- Optional: fresh vegetables such as lettuce, strips of cucumber or bell pepper

DIRECTIONS:

- Drizzle or spread the mustard over the bottom half of the tortilla.
- Lay the roast beef, cheese, and vegetables (if using) evenly over the mustard.
- Starting at the bottom, roll the tortilla up to the top.
- Slice in half and serve.

NUTRIENT	CALORIES	PROTEIN	CARBOHYDRATES	FAT	FIBRE	SODIUM
PER PORTION	183 kcal	13g	11g	9g	2g	329mg

Tuna Sushi

1 PORTION

PREP TIME: 15 minutes | **TOTAL TIME:** 15 minutes

INGREDIENTS:

- 1 sheet nori
- ⅓ cup brown sushi rice, cooked
- 1 tsp (5 mL) low sodium soy sauce
- 1 Tbsp. 2% plain Greek yogurt
- 1/4 can (30 g) low sodium tuna, drained
- 2 Tbsp. red bell pepper, thinly sliced into matchsticks
- 2 Tbsp. cucumber, thinly sliced into matchsticks

DIRECTIONS:

- Lay a bamboo sushi mat or tea towel on a clean flat surface and cover with a layer of plastic wrap to keep it clean.
- Lay the piece of nori on the plastic wrap.
- Spread the rice from left to right from one edge of the nori to the other, leaving an inch gap at the bottom and top. Drizzle the soy sauce over the rice.
- Mix together the Greek yogurt and tuna, then spoon over the rice.
- Layer on the red bell pepper and cucumber.
- Starting from the bottom, fold the mat over, pull back slightly towards you, then continue to roll and pull back to keep the roll tight, until the roll is complete.
- Remove the plastic wrap and mat or towel.
- With a wet knife, slice the sushi into rounds.

NUTRIENT	CALORIES	PROTEIN	CARBOHYDRATES	FAT	FIBRE	SODIUM
PER PORTION	146 kcal	15g	18g	1g	2g	234mg

Tuna Melt Stuffed Tomatoes

1 PORTION

PREP TIME: 5 minutes |  **TOTAL TIME:** 15 minutes

INGREDIENTS:

- 1 large tomato
- 1/4 can (30 g) low sodium tuna, drained
- 1 Tbsp. 2% plain Greek yogurt
- 1 tsp dried dill
- 1 tsp (5 mL) lemon juice
- 1 Tbsp. low fat mozzarella cheese, shredded

DIRECTIONS:

- Preheat oven to 400°F (200°C). Line a baking sheet with foil.
- Slice of the top of the tomato and hollow out inside with a spoon, then roughly chop the insides.
- In a bowl, mix together the inner part of the tomato with the remaining ingredients.
- Spoon the mixture back into the tomato.
- Place the tomato on the baking sheet and bake for 10 minutes to soften the tomato and melt the cheese.

NUTRIENT	CALORIES	PROTEIN	CARBOHYDRATES	FAT	FIBRE	SODIUM
PER PORTION	117 kcal	16g	9g	2g	2g	91mg

Baked Chicken Taquitos

4 PORTIONS

PREP TIME: 15 minutes | **TOTAL TIME:** 50 minutes

INGREDIENTS:

- 8 oz (227 g) raw boneless skinless chicken breast
- ¼ cup 2% cream cheese, softened to room temperature
- 2 Tbsp. partly skimmed mozzarella cheese, shredded
- 1 medium green onion, thinly sliced
- ⅛ tsp black pepper
- 1 tsp chili powder
- ½ tsp ground cumin
- ¼ tsp garlic powder
- 4 5-inch (13 cm) soft corn tortillas
- 1 large egg, beaten

DIRECTIONS:

- Preheat oven to 400°F (200°C). Line one baking sheet with foil and one with parchment paper.
- Place chicken breast on parchment-lined baking sheet. Bake for 18-20 minutes or until chicken is cooked through. Shred chicken using two forks; set aside.
- In a medium bowl, mix together chicken, cream cheese, mozzarella, green onion, black pepper, chili powder, cumin, and garlic powder.
- Warm the tortillas in the microwave for about 20 seconds to help prevent them from cracking.
- Spoon about ¼ cup of the filling onto the centre of each tortilla and roll them up, leaving the ends open.
- Brush the tops of the rolls with egg.
- Place the taquitos seam side down on the foil-lined baking sheet.
- Bake for about 15 minutes, flipping halfway through, or until taquitos are crispy and slightly brown.

NUTRIENT	CALORIES	PROTEIN	CARBOHYDRATES	FAT	FIBRE	SODIUM
PER PORTION	147 kcal	16g	8g	6g	1g	151mg

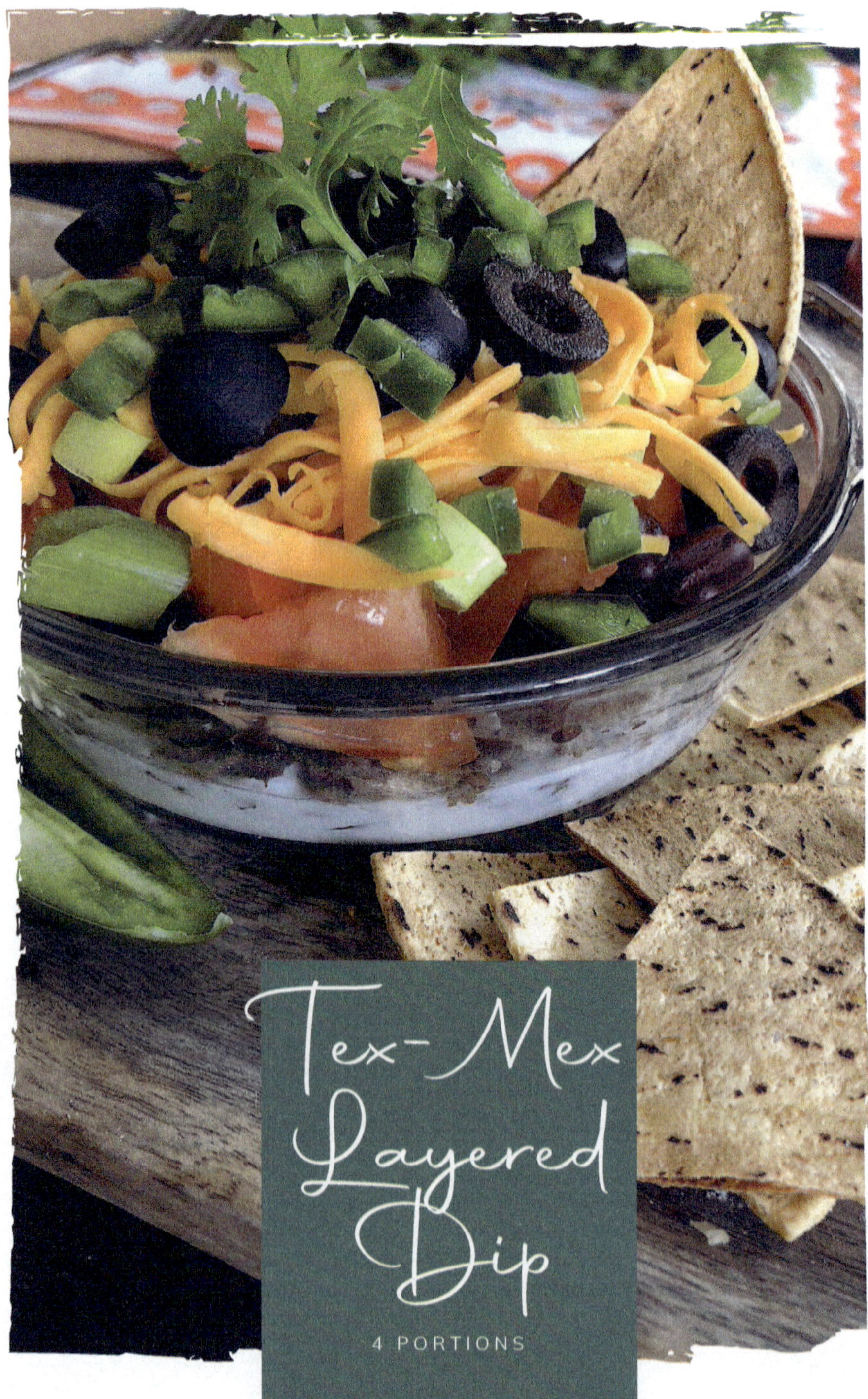

Tex-Mex Layered Dip

4 PORTIONS

 **PREP TIME:** 15 minutes |  **TOTAL TIME:** 40 minutes

INGREDIENTS:

- 4 5-inch (13 cm) soft corn tortillas
- 2.5 oz (70 g) raw extra-lean ground beef
- ¼ cup plain 2% Greek yogurt
- 1 Tbsp. fresh cilantro, chopped
- 1 Tbsp. (15 mL) lime juice
- ⅛ tsp ground cumin
- ½ cup canned no sodium added black beans, drained and rinsed
- 2 medium tomato, finely chopped
- 2 medium green onions, sliced
- ¼ cup low fat cheddar cheese, shredded
- 2 Tbsp. canned black olives, sliced
- 1 Tbsp. jalapeño, finely chopped

DIRECTIONS:

- Preheat oven to 400°F (200°C). Line a baking sheet with foil.
- Cut the tortillas into wedges and arrange in a single layer. Bake for 10 minutes or until crispy, flipping halfway through. Set aside and allow to cool.
- Cook ground beef in medium skillet over medium heat until no longer pink; drain fat. Remove beef from skillet; set aside.
- Mix together the Greek yogurt, cilantro and lime juice; spread over the bottom of a large bowl or container.
- Combine ground beef and cumin and spoon over Greek yogurt mixture.
- Layer on black beans, tomato, and then green onion.
- Finish by sprinkling the cheese, black olives and jalapeño over the top.
- Serve with tortilla chips for dipping.

NUTRIENT	CALORIES	PROTEIN	CARBOHYDRATES	FAT	FIBRE	SODIUM
PER PORTION	132 kcal	11g	15g	3g	3g	109mg

Deviled Eggs

1 PORTION

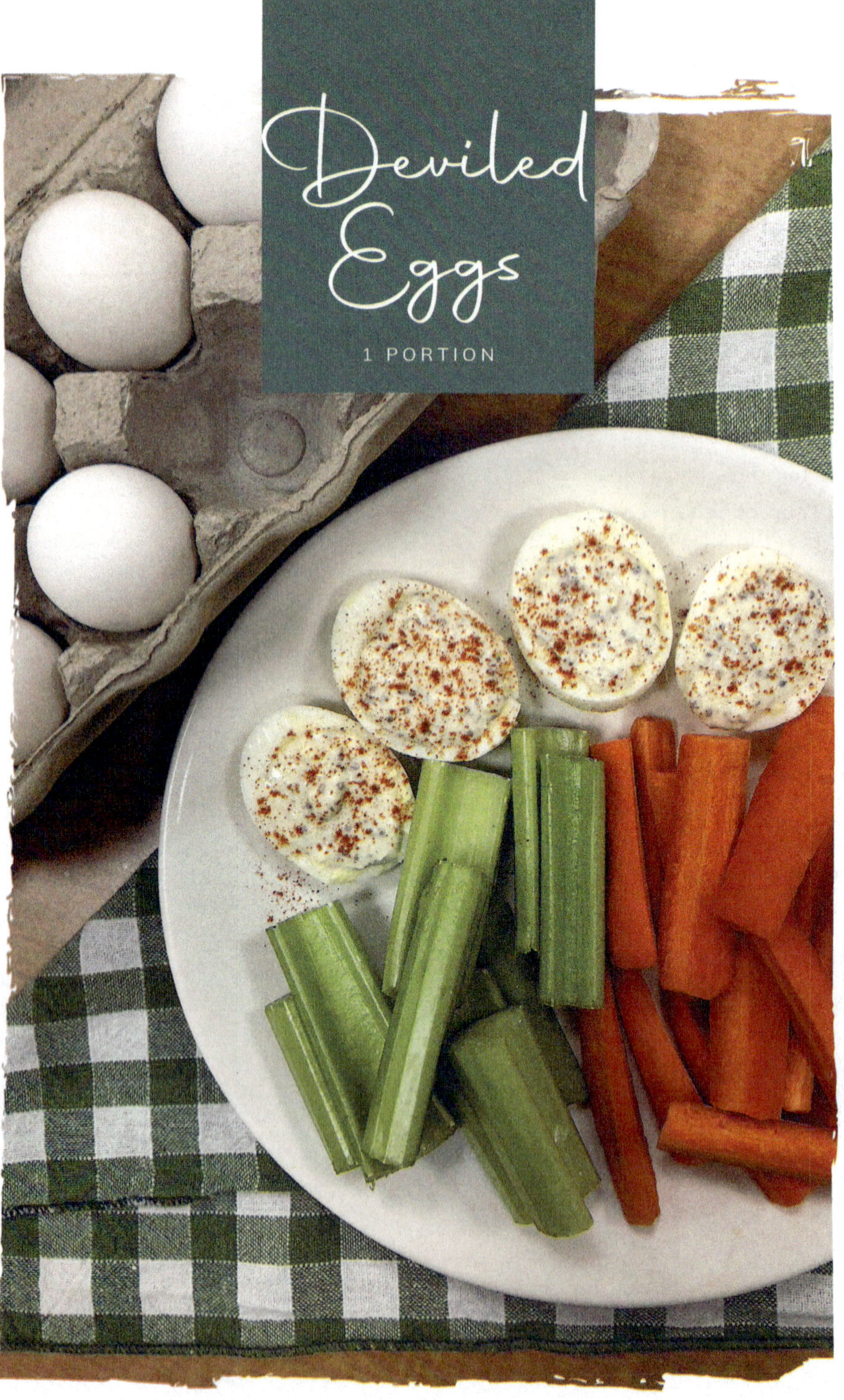

PREP TIME: 5 minutes |  **TOTAL TIME:** 5 minutes

INGREDIENTS:

- 2 large hard-boiled eggs, peeled
- ¼ cup plain 2% Greek yogurt
- ⅛ tsp paprika
- 1 tsp (5 mL) Dijon mustard
- 1 tsp (5 mL) lemon juice

SIDES:

- 1 medium celery stalk
- 1 medium carrot

DIRECTIONS:

- Slice the eggs in half lengthwise.
- Using a spoon, remove the egg yolk from the egg white.
- In a bowl, mix together the egg yolk, Greek yogurt, paprika, Dijon mustard and lemon juice.
- Spoon mixture back into the egg white.
- Slice the celery and carrot into sticks and serve with the deviled eggs.

NUTRIENT PER PORTION	CALORIES	PROTEIN	CARBOHYDRATES	FAT	FIBRE	SODIUM
	229 kcal	18g	12g	12g	2g	346mg

Chicken Skewers with Tzatziki

1 PORTION

PREP TIME: 10 minutes |

TOTAL TIME: 20 minutes

INGREDIENTS:

- 2 wooden or metal skewers
- 1 tsp (5 mL) canola oil
- 4 oz (113 g) raw boneless skinless chicken breast, cubed
- 8 grape tomatoes
- ¼ red onion, cut in half horizontally, and separated into pieces

TZATZIKI:

- ½ cup 2% plain Greek yogurt
- 2 Tbsp. cucumber, diced
- 1 garlic clove, minced
- ½ tsp dried dill
- 1 tsp (5 mL) lemon juice

DIRECTIONS:

- If using, place wooden skewers in a bowl of cold water to soak.
- Brush grill or grill pan lightly with oil and preheat to medium heat.
- Mix together tzatziki ingredients in a small bowl; set aside.
- Remove wooden skewers from water or take metal skewers and thread alternating pieces of chicken, tomato and onion pieces.
- Grill skewers for 5 minutes per side or until chicken is cooked through.
- Serve skewers with tzatziki.

NUTRIENT	CALORIES	PROTEIN	CARBOHYDRATES	FAT	FIBRE	SODIUM
PER PORTION	147 kcal	18g	7g	5g	1g	49mg

Colourful Pasta Salad

4 PORTIONS

 **PREP TIME:** 10 minutes |  **TOTAL TIME:** 2 hours and 20 minutes

INGREDIENTS:

- 6 oz (170 g) dry whole wheat rotini pasta
- 2 Tbsp. (30 mL) olive oil, divided
- 8 oz (227 g) raw boneless skinless chicken breast, chopped
- 1 cup broccoli florets
- ½ cup carrots, cut into coins
- 1 cup red bell pepper, chopped
- ½ small red onion, thinly sliced
- 1 cup sugar snap peas, sliced
- ¼ tsp black pepper
- 1 tsp dried basil
- 1 tsp (5 mL) Dijon mustard
- 2 Tbsp. (30 mL) red wine vinegar

DIRECTIONS:

- Cook the pasta al dente according to package directions. Drain and transfer to a large bowl.
- Heat 1 Tbsp. oil in a medium skillet over medium heat.
- Cook chicken for 4-5 minutes, stirring occasionally, until cooked through. Set aside.
- Steam broccoli and carrots for 3-4 minutes or until tender crisp. Add red bell pepper, red onion, peas, and chicken to the pasta.
- Mix 1 Tbsp. oil, black pepper, basil, Dijon mustard, and red wine vinegar in a small bowl.
- Pour the dressing over the pasta salad and mix well.
- Cover and refrigerate for at least 2 hours or overnight before serving.

NUTRIENT	CALORIES	PROTEIN	CARBOHYDRATES	FAT	FIBRE	SODIUM
PER PORTION	156 kcal	10g	18g	5g	4g	44mg

Greek Yogurt Popsicles

2 PORTIONS

PREP TIME: 5 minutes |

TOTAL TIME: 6 hours

INGREDIENTS:

- 1 cup plain 2% Greek yogurt
- 1 cup strawberries, or fruit of choice*

DIRECTIONS:

- Blend the Greek yogurt and strawberries in a blender or food processor on high speed until smooth.
- Pour mixture into popsicle molds or small paper cups.
- Freeze for 2 hours, then insert popsicle sticks 1 inch (2.5 cm) into molds.
- Freeze for 4-6 hours or overnight.
- Run the mold under hot water to easily remove popsicles.

*Note: Nutrient analysis done with strawberries.

NUTRIENT PER PORTION	CALORIES	PROTEIN	CARBOHYDRATES	FAT	FIBRE	SODIUM
	110 kcal	12g	10g	3g	2g	60mg

Very Berry Smoothie

2 PORTIONS

PREP TIME: 5 minutes |  **TOTAL TIME:** 5 minutes

INGREDIENTS:

- ½ cup (125 mL) 2% milk
- 1 cup plain 2% Greek yogurt
- 1 cup fresh spinach
- 1 cup frozen mixed berries

DIRECTIONS:

- Pour milk into blender, followed by Greek yogurt, spinach, and berries.
- Blend until smooth.

NUTRIENT PER PORTION	CALORIES	PROTEIN	CARBOHYDRATES	FAT	FIBRE	SODIUM
	139 kcal	12g	15g	4g	3g	78mg

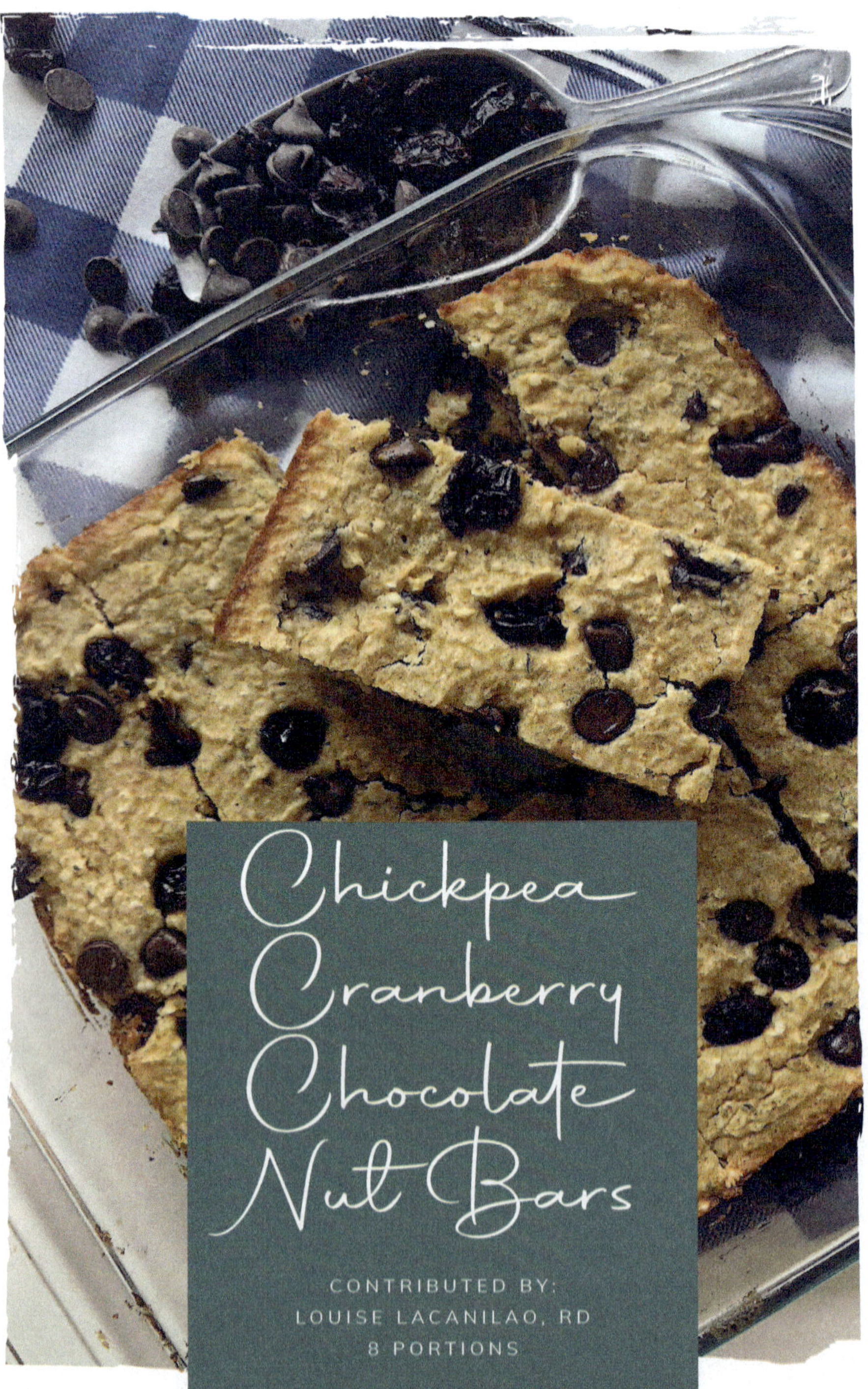

Chickpea Cranberry Chocolate Nut Bars

CONTRIBUTED BY:
LOUISE LACANILAO, RD
8 PORTIONS

PREP TIME: 15 minutes |  **TOTAL TIME:** 40 minutes

INGREDIENTS:

- 1 can (14 oz/398 mL) no sodium added chickpeas, drained and rinsed
- 2 large eggs
- ½ cup natural peanut butter or nut free alternative
- ¼ cup hemp seeds
- ¼ cup (60 mL) honey
- ¼ cup chocolate chips
- ¼ cup dried cranberries
- 1 tsp (5 mL) canola oil

DIRECTIONS:

- Preheat oven to 350°F (175°C).
- Place drained chickpeas in a food processor and blend until a smooth paste is formed.
- Mix together eggs, peanut butter, hemp seeds, and honey in a medium bowl.
- Mix in chickpea paste.
- Fold in the chocolate chips and cranberries.
- Grease an 8 x 8-inch (1.4 L) baking dish with oil and spread the mixture into dish.
- Bake for 25 minutes.
- Leave in the pan to completely cool and firm up before slicing into 8 bars.
- Bars can be stored for up to 2 days on the counter, 1 week in the fridge or 3 months in the freezer.

NUTRIENT	CALORIES	PROTEIN	CARBOHYDRATES	FAT	FIBRE	SODIUM
PER PORTION	280 kcal	11g	31g	14g	4g	84mg

Printed in Great Britain
by Amazon

51297448R00096